A MESSAGE
NOTIFICATION

.

A MESSAGE NOTIFICATION

OUR JOURNEY TO A BEAUTIFUL LOVE STORY

TIMOTHY AND
LAVONICA DAVIS

Published by Truth Publications, LLC
www.truth-brand.com

A Message Notification: Our Journey to a Beautiful Love Story
ISBN: 978-1-7366112-5-8
Copyright ©2022 by Timothy and Lavonica Davis
Cover Concept: Lavonica Davis
www.timandlavonica.com
(870) 460-5130

To all the people who still believe in Biblical truth, that marriage is between a man and woman, and that God blesses that kind of union.

To all the people who know that love is real and attainable, and that God is still authoring love stories....

Table of Contents

Acknowledgments

To God, the Lord Jesus Christ, to whom we give all honor and glory; without Him authoring this story, this divine encounter would have not started.

To our children: Stephanie "Lady" Smith, Jewan Davis, Katlyn Penn, Isaiah Davis, Bianca Watson, Makayla Watson, Ahmod Davis, and Monica Davis. They have experienced all the good, bad, happy, and sad moments. We love each of you and appreciate the dedication and role you played in keeping our blended family a family. Our son-in-law, Chris Smith, and grandchildren, Aleyah Davis and Kennedy Smith for just being who you are to us.

To our parents: Marion Davis (Tim's mother) and Kenneth and Gladys Tidwell (Lavonica's father and deceased mother). We have learned a great deal from you each teaching and raising us in the true knowledge of God. Grandma Sue Ella (Tim's deceased grandmother), raised him to know the meaning of mercy, grace, and unconditional love. Johnny C. Davis (Tim's father), who didn't get it right at first, has come along and shown Tim a father's love, and who now loves his grandchildren so much.

To our siblings and their spouses: Sabrina Malone, Calvin and Charmaine Tidwell, Stephanie Robinson, Christi and Steve Mack, Teresa and Corey Robinson, Tywana Tidwell, and Kelvin and Tiffany Tidwell. Thank you for all the encouraging words, laughter, and acceptance of the will of God in our lives.

◆ ◆ ◆

To everyone who made this book possible and helped make our vision come true:

We thank Timothy Johnson with Truth Publication, LLC for his diligence and thorough assistance with this book. He showed us how to streamline this process so our book would be successful.

Many thanks to Bethany Gallimore, Freelance Editor, and former Writing Instructor at the Arkansas State University at Jonesboro, who worked with perfection. She played a major role in the beginning process with editing our book.

We thank Apostle Keith Marks and Dr. Claudette Marks for their mentorship, friendship, and always having a *rhema* word and showing us the next level God has for us.

We thank Apostle Amos L. Howard, Yolanda Howard, and the Living Trust Family for being great people and our pastoral family. They challenge our thinking and catapult us to reach that next level in the kingdom. We know, "It does matter where you go to church!"

To Pastor Joseph L. Mosley and Lady Cynthia Mosley, the great pastor and wife of Holy Hill Church of God in Christ in Banks, Arkansas. You all took out so much time and molded and covered Tim in his relationship with God. May everything you touch be blessed.

Thanks to Daniel and Toya Glover, our RVPs. You are coaching and teaching us the keys to becoming a successful couple in business. Thanks for being our mentors and friends. You are the epitome that great rewards come to those who work smarter and not harder.

To all the people who still believe in Biblical truth, that marriage is between a man and woman, and God blesses that kind of union.

To all the people who believe in marriage—we didn't say a perfect marriage, but a perfecting marriage. It is a daily walk of understanding, grace, patience, caring, and most of all, love.

Introduction

Many of us love a good love story, whether in a movie, on television, or in reality. No matter how much evil is in the world, love still covers a multitude of sins. For a good love story to be successful, it needs a man, a woman, background, hope, and most of all love. We believe no matter how many years pass, love stories will continue to be told, as long as there are humans to tell them.

The important question is, "what is love?" If a person were to Google the word *love*, about 14,600,000,000 results would be available. However, one of the best definitions of love is summed up in Corinthians:

> Love is patient and kind. Love is not jealous or boastful or proud or rude. It does not demand its own way. It is not irritable, and it keeps no record of being wronged. It does not rejoice about injustice but rejoices whenever the truth wins out. Love never gives up, never loses faith, is always hopeful, and endures through every circumstance.
>
> 1 Cor. 13: 4-7

We are not naive to the fact that love cannot pay the bills. However, love is needed to make a relationship work. It is like Apostle Amos Howard always said, "Love always seeks to give the advantage." There are times during relationships when it gets tough, and the thoughts of leaving scream louder than the thoughts of staying. We have experienced both the good and bad sides of relationships. The conclusion we reached was that love is a journey. Our definition of love, our upbringing, and previous relationships played a major role in creating our beautiful love story.

LAVONICA'S STORY: I had one of the greatest experiences as a little girl: being raised by my biological dad and mom. I had three older sisters and one younger brother, all raised in the same household as me. However, my older sister wasn't my dad's biological child. My mom was pregnant when they met, so it was still like she was my dad's child. He never showed indifference. Also, my dad had another son who was being raised by his grandparents. This was a little weird at first because we were not all in the same house, but we didn't have any choice but to accept the fact.

From a little girl's perceptive, my dad and mom were happy. They gave us a stable home and consistency. I don't remember a whole lot of arguing. When they would disagree, Daddy would say, "Shut up, Gladys!", and that would be the end of the disagreement. I can truly say my momma mastered how to hold her peace and (as the church people say) let the Lord fight her battle. Seriously, I got my first lessons on relationships from them. They both worked; momma did the cooking and daddy did the outside work such as taking care of the yard and washing the cars. Neither one of them did the cleaning though; we (the kids) had to do that part. Everyone had their roles to play. They raised us in a God-fearing home, and despite spending a lot of time in church, our family seemed to have a very balanced life.

My parents' love for each other was noticed by the community. I felt they were the epitome of what marriage was supposed to be. My momma always made us respect our dad. I remember some advice she gave me a long time ago. She said, "Vonna, take care of your husband. Put him before those kids because your kids will leave you, but your husband will be the person to be there for you." Life is ironic because those same words came back to test my momma later in life.

My dad loved my momma. If he could have given her the world, he would have. I am not saying they were perfect, but as a kid, it sure did seem that way. Everyone knew that Kenneth DeWayne Tidwell, my dad, took care of Gladys Mae Tidwell, my mom. He was a great provider; went to work and paid the bills. I can count on one hand the days my dad took off work. He went to work when he was sick and many days when he was tired. I wanted a man like my daddy; one who was a provider. My mom was a hard worker, also. Year after year, they would sacrifice by working in factories to make sure we had food, shelter, and clothing.

When I was in the fifth grade, my parents bought a new full-sized van. It seemed life was getting better for us financially, but it was one of the worst times of my life. During that time, I saw less and less of my momma. She was either gone somewhere or at work. It was just dad, my siblings, and I going to church all the time. Before we knew it, momma started living a different lifestyle which we were not used to seeing. Eventually, she decided what she felt was best for her and her happiness was for her to move out.

Our happy family was no longer a happy family. It didn't take long for my parents to get a divorce. My two older siblings, Christi and Teresa, moved in with my momma and her new boyfriend. He was younger than her and an abusive alcoholic. My other siblings (Tywana and Kelvin) and I stayed with daddy. He did not stay single long. A new lady came to our church, someone played matchmaker, and they eventually got married.

Our daddy's new wife (or as we used to call her, "the devil's sister") was a wolf in sheep's clothing. She had five kids of her own, and it didn't take long before her true nature was revealed. She was not as devout of a Christin in private as she portrayed to be in public. Eventually, her public façade dissipated, and her rude, manipulative personality appeared. Her negative influence even had its effect on dad. He eventually stopped going to church, stopped reading his bible, and stopped doing many of the positive things he normally would do. It was heartbreaking to see this great man of God and former deacon in the church veer so far from God – as well as veering away from the values he instilled in us. It had gotten so bad that Tywana, Kelvin, and I ended up living with momma and her boyfriend, which wasn't much better. It took a mental toll on me to see my parents do the very things they taught us against.

Despite it all, a few years later, my parents fell back in love and remarried. My dad used to say, "If she try to leave me this time, I'm going to trip her." That second time around was sweeter than the first. I hate they had to go through all of that, but they came out as better individuals. So, my understanding of love and relationships was that true love could always be restored and amended.

As a child I said, when I get married, I would never cheat on my husband. It was always my desire, also, that my husband and I would raise our children together, until death do us part. I have seen firsthand the heartbreak cheating can have on a family, and I didn't want that for my children. Living through separation and renewal, however, is how I developed my loyalty for marriage.

◆ ◆ ◆

TIM'S STORY: As far back as I can remember, it has always been just my mom and me. So, my depiction of how a husband is supposed to love a wife did not come from my home, but from outside my home. My only models were my aunties and uncles' marriages or those on television. Growing up, my mom never had another man live with us.

My mom had me when she was 16 years old. Since she was young, my grandmother, Sue Ella, and my aunties helped my mom raise me. My dad, Johnny, married my mom when I was 5 months old. Their relationship was turbulent, to say the least. He would drink and become abusive toward her. Mom reassured me that she tried to make the marriage work; however, she reached a breaking point and left with me.

Throughout my young life, my dad didn't do his part for me. Every so often, he would pick me up to take me to his house. However, he would soon leave, and I would end up with his sisters and his mother watching me. I don't know why he didn't get involved in my life. I can remember many birthdays and Christmases passing without a call or a gift. As I grew up, I got used to it and made up in my mind that when I had kids, I would love them and take good care of them. In all honesty, I learned what not to do from him.

I thought that the pain of not having a father figure would bypass me. However, as a teen, I became another victim of having daddy issues. My life began a downward spiral, and I was making bad decisions. My decisions got me a bed at Camp Robinson Youth Challenge Program in Little Rock. I was kicked out of school for my behavior and someone else had to show me how to develop my self-control and deal with the void I had.

I graduated from Camp Robinson and was able to go back to school as a senior at Hermitage High School. Due to being at Camp Robinson, I was behind in school. Determined to catch up, I got focused and worked double to graduate high school earning a 3.2 GPA. I wanted to make my mom and grandmother proud of me. By this time, because of my grandmother Sue Ella's love for God, my mom had given her life to God. My mom became the sounding board I needed to look beyond the past, forgive, and love my dad. My mother showed me that she could make it as a single parent. It took being strong-willed, strong-minded, and having a lot of love. I never got the chance to see my mom in love with a man, but she did teach me how to love and care for people, which is priceless.

Chapter 1

Writing Backwards

There are times in life when finding love seems to be for other people or just a fictional storyline in a movie. However, we have experienced its reality. It is not enough to say or hear those three words, "I love you;" there must be a meaning behind them. We are no experts, but no one can take away our story. A story we can truly say that we are only the narrators of, but we give God the glory and credit for authoring this beautiful love story.

LAVONICA'S STORY: The year was 2010. I was thirty-two years old, married, and had three beautiful daughters: Stephanie, whom we always called Lady, twelve years old; Bianca, eight; and Makayla, four. We just moved to an apartment in Baton Rouge, Louisiana—it was our eighth time moving in our marriage of ten years. Life with my husband Fred had been turbulent. Getting married at age twenty-two with a two-year-old going into the relationship was not a traditional Biblical start to a marriage, especially one that would be approved in a household affiliated with the COGIC (Church of God in Christ) church. However, Fred accepted my daughter as his own; but he, too, brought something in addition to his love for me into the marriage. He had an ex-wife and two children as well.

When we moved to Baton Rouge, a fresh start for us was all I could think about. We always had financial problems and personal setbacks. Every house we rented, we got evicted from. I remember one landlord left a note on the front door which said, "Beg, borrow, or steal, I want my money!" It kind of tickles me now, but at that time, it was not funny at all. However, that was not the most embarrassing moment. We did not have enough money to pay our gas bill, and I was too prideful to ask anyone else for assistance. So, we managed to deal with not having gas. This was during the winter months too! The house was very insulated, so we would heat the house with our electric stove oven and boil water mixed with some cold water to take baths. All the while thinking I am going through trials and

tribulations in the name of the Lord. The embarrassing part came when the gas was off so long, they took the gas meter off the house. We lived on a corner lot so everyone could see it was missing. My mom pulled up in the driveway and asked, "Vonna, where in the world is your gas meter?" Full of regret, I told her the truth. She gave us the money, and we were able to get the gas back on.

Before and after of the gas meter at our house in Hope, AR

It's a good thing that this story and many other stories similar to that story are in our past. My parents could not understand why I would move to another state with a person who had shown that he was incapable of being a provider, incapable of taking care of me and my children. But me being me, I was optimistic about our future. Well, it did not take long before the eventual happened; we had to move again. We had only been in the apartment in Baton Rouge for six months. He had gotten "laid off" from his work in road construction. The eviction notice was left on the door giving us the ultimatum of paying the last two months of rent that were owed or moving out. With our financial state, we had no choice but to move.

With rent being cheaper on the other side of town, we ended up there. It was not the best neighborhood, however. The high crime rate, inadequate school systems, and impoverishment dominated the area. However, there were bright spots despite the move. Stephanie was accepted into a gifted and talented school, and I found a job working as a receptionist at an independent living apartment complex. Being away from my family helped me to see the reality of my situation. I had always been a praying woman; I had been waiting on God to help us and deliver us. However, I came to the realization that deliverance was not going to happen with this particular guy. I had put so much time into this marriage and still had the same results. I began to long for what I had in the past with my high school sweetheart, Chris. He had money, and he used to spoil me. While on my job, I began to search for him online, basically searching for something different. In the meantime, we got evicted again. However, this time we did not have an alternative. I didn't want my parents involved; I didn't want them to hear how bad things had become. So, we ended up homeless, but only for a few hours. The church we attended gave us some money for a hotel until we could get paid, and Fred started working at the construction job again. We stayed at Microtel for one month until we got our income tax refund. Finally, we were able to rent a home.

I was physically, spiritually, mentally, and emotionally tired, and I started daydreaming of the day I could finally be happy. I was not sure how I could possibly be a "Woman of God" and leave my husband. My relationship with God began to get shaky. I felt trapped, lonely, and depressed. I felt like I had no way out. "How can I get out," I would wonder. We could not afford the house we stayed in, so we did what we did best...packed and left. This time, Fred met a couple who offered to pay for our rent and security deposit. Despite the narrow save, I knew I did not want to spend another year like this.

My girls deserved better. I told them that the way we had been living was not normal. In November 2011, we had been staying at that house for two weeks. I called my parents and told them the girls and I were moving back home to Arkansas. My dad said the words I knew meant forgiveness and acceptance: "Baby, you can always come home." Early that Tuesday morning, I waited until Fred went to work, then packed all my clothes and my girls' clothes that could fit in the trunk of my 2005 Cadillac Deville (a car my parents gave us for free). I wrote a note and left it on the dining room table. I had made up my mind that I was leaving my husband of 11 years.

For a moment, doubts filled my head, but I remembered the words of a friend: whenever you make a well-thought-out decision to do something— stick to it! This thought catapulted me into keeping the commitment I made to myself to leave. I used the last bit of money I had to fill my car up with gas, and I headed back home to Arkansas.

> *Whenever you make a well-thought-out decision to do something-stick to it!*

♦ ♦ ♦

TIM'S STORY: The year was 2007. Christy and I had finally gotten married, after being together "off and on" for nine years. See, our story was a little complicated, by the way. We had a son, Jewan, in 2000; but eventually, we went our separate ways. A couple of years passed, and she got pregnant with Isaiah by someone else. However, before Isaiah was born, we were back together. In 2006, Ahmod was born and a couple of years later Monica came into this world. Owning multiple clothing stores, vacationing, and having money: that was our lifestyle. Life was good and was getting better; we were a team. Christy was my "ride or die."

I would have described our relationship during that time as what people would call a *power couple*. I was married to my best friend. Christy was very supportive, and we were all about *making that money*. I didn't have to worry about anything because I knew she had my back. I was glad that we decided to do things the right way.

In 2007, I gave my life to God, and she did too. God was at the center of our relationship and going to church at Holy Hill Church of God in Christ was a norm. We answered the call of God on our lives to preach the gospel, and we began a ministry right in our home, accompanied by our children: Jewan, who was ten; Isaiah, eight; Ahmod, four; and Monica, two. The ministry had grown and there were many opportunities to proclaim the word of God.

Oh, but how time brought about a change. I saw it coming slowly: the change of heart, the love for God, and her love for me. The differences in our beliefs began fracturing our marriage. We stopped our ministry and decided to go back to Holy Hill. She attended for a few months but then decided to start going to another church, which caused everything to shift. Neither one of us were perfect, but I tried my best to make everything work. The more I tried, the more I pushed her away. It got to a point where she no longer attended church. She went back to her old ways of living and began to act as if she was single again. She was tired of the saved, holy lifestyle which we had come accustomed to, and she wanted to revert to our old ways of living. However, the part that hurt me the most was when she called me boring. She said that she missed "kicking it" and the good times we used to have together.

In December 2011, we moved to Hot Springs, Arkansas, hoping this would help our marriage. We felt a new town, a new scenery, would be best for us. It didn't take long before I felt like I was losing my family and losing my mind. *Where do I go from here*, I would ask myself. It did not take long for that question to be answered by her. It was February 20, 2012, a day I will never forget. I came home from work to find that she had moved out. Her heart had been gone for a while; now her body finally followed. She had taken everything except the salt and pepper  shakers, which would have been taken if she could have reached them in the top cabinet. She took Isaiah and Monica with her and left Jewan and Ahmod with me. My family was torn apart, something that I never thought would happen. I had invested so much time and energy into our family. My dad was not a part of my life, and I did not want the same fate for my children.

There is always a background story to love. A background story is a piece that makes up the big picture. Why people do what they do and say what they say can be answered by learning the background story. People just do not become who they are overnight; it is situations, problems, pains, and hurts that make a person become who they are. The commonality in those experiences is what brings people together.

Chapter 2

Tried, Tired, and Transitions

Life can leave us blindsided by unexpected, seemly unprepared moments. One can rest assured that life goes on, the clock does not stop ticking, and the sunrises and sunsets do not stop. The question is, how to move on and move forward when it feels life has stopped? What is next when you did not know there would be a next? Lastly, where is God in all of this?

LAVONICA'S STORY: *"Buzz," "buzz," "buzz,"* I looked at my phone; it was him texting me. He had no clue that the girls and I were on our way to Arkansas. I said to myself that I would get further away before I respond. An hour later, *"buzz," "buzz," "buzz,"* it was him texting again, asking how my day was going. I didn't know what to say, my brain was frozen. Then my phone rang; it was him. I took a deep breath and answered. I nerved up the guts to tell him that I left, and I was on my way to Arkansas with the girls. The only thing I remember was how my ears muffled his words before they reached my brain. To me, he sounded like the cartoon Charlie Brown, *"Wah wah wah"* and *"wah wah wah."* It didn't really matter what he said. I was gone and had no intentions of going back. I was far enough that he could not catch me.

The whole drive back to Arkansas, I couldn't help but think of what those eleven years consisted of, the good and the bad. I wasn't the perfect wife, but I wasn't the worst either. I put a lot of time and energy into crying, wishing, praying, and hoping that

> *The hope of something better screamed louder at me.*

our life together would improve. However, the hope of something better screamed louder at me.

I begin to finely comb through our marriage to see what had happened. While it is not worth talking about when we first met, I would love to describe him. He was 5'4", a short but very confident and attractive man. He was a smooth talker. My momma used to say that he could sell shoes to a person with no feet, and he could sell ice to an Eskimo. He had so many dreams and goals that he wanted to achieve—but that was the problem, too many dreams and goals, so he never got around to any of them. He became a Minister and then an Elder during our marriage. However, like many people who haven't dealt with their secrets, the spirits behind those secrets dealt with him.

I must admit, he did love me and the girls; he just didn't know how to be a husband and father, to protect and provide for his family. Living life with him was a roller coaster ride: he could go from working three jobs to no work at all for three months. So, we were always playing catch-up. He owed just about all my family members money, and he would pawn anything of value we owned, including jewelry he had given me. There were so many "broke" days in which not even a penny could be found in our house. I stayed as long as I did because I wanted the girls to have what I had growing up: a mom and dad in the home. However, I believe that our relationship and living situation was so toxic, it wasn't even worth it anymore.

After driving, thinking, and crying, I finally made it to Arkansas. I was so happy to be home! I felt a great burden lifted off me. My parents hugged the girls and welcomed us back. They didn't ask me too many questions, and I didn't volunteer much information either. I tried my best to shield anything that had happened during my marriage from my parents, or better yet, anyone. However, I believe they knew more than I thought they knew.

I was back home, and I knew our lives were about to change. I didn't know what our future looked like, or what I was going to do next. That move didn't come with a well-thought-out plan. The only expectation I had was finally being happy one day.

The next day, reality hit me. I was back in Arkansas living with my parents. My sister, who was divorced, her three children, and my niece who was pregnant all lived there as well, which was a total of eleven people in a three-bedroom, double-wide mobile home. At

The only expectation I had was finally being HAPPY ONE DAY.

that moment, I didn't care; I was glad to be free from living in poverty for eleven years. I began getting my life together spiritually, emotionally, and physically. I was praying more, forgiving the past hurts, and moving forward. I was faithfully attending my previous church home, Faith Temple Church of

God in Christ, where my dad and mom were the pastor and wife. Lastly, I was committed to exercising regularly and eating healthy every day.

Life had already gotten better for me in that short amount of time. Within 5 months, I had a job, not my dream job, but I was able to save some money to get the girls and me an apartment one day.

The girls were doing well in school, they had readjusted quickly. I was a little concerned about Makayla because she was a daddy's girl. However, with so many people in the house, her mind was kept occupied. I never thought I would have to say these next few words, but I was learning how to be a single mom. Being back around family brought me great healing and happiness. I felt like a new person.

My new normal meant getting up at 4:00 a.m. to get ready for work. Bianca and Makayla slept in the bed with me. I would have their clothes laid out for them to wear to school each weekday. Lady, showing true oldest-sibling responsibility, made sure they got on the bus for school. I drove to work about thirty minutes away, got in my eight hours, and made it home around 3:30 p.m. Every day when I got home from work, my momma—Gladys, had dinner ready for everyone in the house. The older children would be home and were talking about school and things that saw on Facebook, mainly.

My sister, Tywana, was an avid Facebook user. She had over 1,000 friends at that time. I had created a Facebook page a couple of years prior but didn't see any significance in it. However, all those conversations about Facebook got me curious; I felt I was missing out on so much that was happening not being on Facebook.

◆ ◆ ◆

TIM'S STORY: I was blindsided. What had just happened? I was left alone with my thoughts: "Did she really just leave?" – "Am I a single parent now?"—"Do I just let this be, or do I fight for our marriage?"—"I have invested too much time and money in this relationship; do I want to do this alone?" I had so many thoughts and emotions running through my mind. However, the main thought that kept screaming at me was how I just wanted to be happy!

I knew I could have made it without her, but I didn't want to. I wasn't ready to let it go. We had accomplished so many great things in our marriage. We owned four clothing and shoe stores, went on many memorable vacations, got our licenses to open a group home, and I was still hopeful about having a ministry together. We had already broken up and gotten back together many times before; but I knew, if this wasn't rectified quickly, there would be no coming back from this one.

Despite what just took place, I wasn't settled on our partnership being over yet. I had big plans for our lives. We were supposed to do life together.

Hours passed and the reality started to clear up my confusion. It was not a dream; she was gone! She split the kids down the middle as she left: my two and her two. I had to work the next day. "Who would watch Jewan and Ahmod?" I thought.

I had so many thoughts and emotions running through my mind. However, the main thought that kept screaming at me was how I just wanted to be happy!

I had no family that lived in Hot Springs. The other big problem was we had no beds, no living room set, no pots and pans, no table, and no food. We had to make pallets on the floor that night. We had to do what we had to do.

After the chaos settled, I had to have a real conversation with my boys. I reminded them that we were going to make it. What I came to realize very quickly was that life goes on.

I would continue to go to work to make sure we have a roof over our heads, food in the refrigerator, gas to get to work, and lights on in the house. However, when I was not at work, I spent as much time with the boys as possible to keep our minds off what was going on. We wrestled, played video games, and played basketball together. I relied on Jewan a great deal to help me with Ahmod. I tried my best to hold on to my relationship with God. I found myself looking for answers and directions from Him. I ran more to Him to help me drown out the chaos in my life. The only way I knew how to do this was by going to church more and more. Not only did I seek God about my marriage, but shortly after, I started having trouble with my downstairs neighbor's complaints about us making too much noise. It wasn't just one time, but it was several times. She even threatened to call the police on us. We tried our best to tip-toe around, but they were boys; it was hard on them to keep tiptoeing around all day. It just felt like one drama after the other.

I believe during this time I started losing Jewan. He couldn't understand why his mom would take some and leave some…leave some of her kids, that is. However, Ahmod never voiced that it bothered him. Jewan began to act out; he started smoking cigarettes and fighting at school. I saw this happening, but I was too focused on trying to fix my marriage and take care of the three of us–I guess more physically and not so much emotionally. Instead of talking things out, I just tried to fill the void with fun stuff to do.

When life is real and situations are tough, it is so easy not to see God in it. He feels so far away, even to a point of not being there. In these times of stress, some people give up hope, give up their families, or even give up their lives. However, when we look back on our tough times, God was there the whole time. There are a thousand scenarios that could have taken place in this world due to pressure. All we can say is, but God! He was there through it all. Despite it all, God still has a plan and purpose in mind.

Chapter 3

"Decisions Made Me Do It"

A decision is a conclusion or resolution reached after consideration. We are faced with decisions daily. Even when we choose not to make a decision, we made that decision. Some of us experience life and conclude that a decision was "good" or "bad," but it nonetheless has been made. Consequences always follow. Is it right to get upset with others for the bad decisions we made in life? The best thing about a consequence: it should teach a person a lesson or two. It should become a guardrail for the next decision that is coming.

LAVONICA'S STORY: I updated my profile picture on Facebook. Tywana helped me choose the perfect picture. She informed me that my profile picture was important. It was the first thing people would see. My sister was no novice when it came to social media. Before Facebook, she had a MySpace account. I never did get into that type of stuff. She

The Facebook profile picture 12/2011

was always a social butterfly, though. I followed her lead, slowly. I started liking other people's statues and pictures; I even started posting statues and pictures of my own. Now, I was able to be a part of those conversations with my family about what was going on in the Facebook world.

The months seemed to pass by very quickly. At first, Fred was calling a lot, talking with both me and with the girls. Eventually, however, the phone calls seemed to slow down. I believe he finally got the hint; there was no persuading me back. The sad part was, he even slowed down on calling and talking with the girls. Makayla would always ask to call him. He would talk a little bit to her before asking to speak with me. Lady and Bianca seemed not to care to talk with him anymore. I can remember an incident when Lady decided to try out for the cheerleading team, and she made it. For some reason, cheerleading uniforms were way more expensive than uniforms for other sports. I called Lady's biological dad, Perry, thinking maybe it was time he helped a little. Maybe it was time for him to get involved in her life. He laughed in my face saying that I never called; and now that I did, it was about money. I told him not to worry about it. I called Fred and asked him for help. He would only give me the money on the condition that I told him that I loved him. I did not want to, and although I said it anyway, I did not mean it. He, then, gave me half of the expense. At that moment, I saw how easy it can be for single moms to get caught up in doing things they normally wouldn't do for their kids.

Living at mom's house gave me the opportunity to look back on the person I was before I met Fred. One day while looking through my senior memory book, I remembered the memories I had with my high school sweetheart, Chris. I began to miss him, dearly. I remembered all the fun we had together and what a great couple we were. It had been fifteen years since we last spoke.

I decided to look for him on Facebook. I checked out his profile picture and a couple more of his pictures. That was short-lived as he only had three pictures posted. I had the option to message him, but I decided not to. I had the phone number of a mutual friend, so I built up some nerves and called her. She said Chris was living back in California and gave me his number. I called him, nervously. I could not believe it; he was actually on the other end of the phone. My heart was racing a hundred miles an hour. So many emotions were taking place within me. Guilt, shame, regret, remorse, but most of all love. Yes! Love at hello. We talked for hours about our past, present, and future. I hung up the phone believing this could be the start of something great! Over the next month, we started calling or texting nearly every day.

However, with this reconnection came tragedy. In August 2012, my mom suffered a massive stroke. I can remember like it was yesterday, the last time I talked to her when she was in her right mind. It was a Saturday morning, and she had been having trouble with her vision and her right wrist. She even ran over a curb while she was driving. She had been talking "out of her head," showing confusion and disorientation. Despite these signs, none of us recognized the symptoms of a stroke. On that Saturday, my aunt, Ann, wasn't feeling well herself. Mom asked me to go buy a fish plate from the church and take it to her. She said, "I got to take care of my sister." I replied with worry: "You all have been trying to take care of each other, but you haven't been feeling well yourself."

The family agreed that momma needed to go to the hospital. Daddy took her in, and that's when we discovered the bad news: Momma had a massive stroke. She started recovering pretty quickly while in ICU, and she eventually was moved to a regular room. She was showing signs of progression as she was talking and eating. One day, however, she just began to sleep all day. The nurse suggested asking a neurologist for an MRI. We did, and the results showed that mom had undergone another massive stroke while in the hospital without anyone realizing it.

My family was a praying family who trusted and believed in God. The family pulled together and was a comfort to one another. Momma was finally released from the hospital and transported to a rehabilitation center.   Now life for me had changed. When I came home, there was no mom. I had to pick up the pieces and make sure the puzzle stayed together. For those weeks, I would get off work, cook for the family, help the kids with their homework, and then go with daddy to visit momma at the rehabilitation center. I would take Bianca and Makayla with me and leave Lady at the house. Not realizing it, I began to limit my parental guidance to Makayla and Bianca, which became one of my biggest regrets. Meanwhile, I was still conversing with Chris. His words of encouragement helped me deal with this situation.

During this time, my divorce from Fred was getting finalized. My oldest sister, Christi, went to court with me for moral support. I remember sharing some stories with the judge about my marriage with Fred. This was my sister's first time hearing it, and she cried like a baby. I was happy for that day; it was a weight that was lifted off of me. I even thought about celebrating my divorce with a post on Facebook, but quickly changed my mind. It just wasn't my style nor my personality. All those months that I talked with Chris while still being officially married to Fred, deep down inside, I knew it was wrong. However, I justified it to myself every time the guilty feelings would come. I had stopped consulting God about my love life and was doing what I wanted to do during that time.

◆ ◆ ◆

TIM'S STORY: I still can't believe I did what I did, but I did it! A couple of weeks had passed since Christy left, and we were still making pallets on the floor. I was passing the apartment dumpster on my way to work, and I saw a queen-sized mattress and box spring still in the plastic beside the dumpster. The pride in me screamed, *"No...what are you about to do?"* However, the necessity screamed louder to see this as a blessing. I made a compromise with myself that if the mattress and box spring were still there when I got off work, I would get them. The first thing I did when I returned to the apartment was drive by the dumpster. They were still there. I took the plastic off the mattress and box spring and put them in my apartment. This had to be one of the lowest points in my life.

Time passed and the boys and I got into a routine. Jewan, Ahmod, and I were managing as a new family unit. In the meantime, I was still trying to get my wife and other kids back home. I continued to call her and just tried to start over as friends to get her back, taking it slow. However, I felt like I was hitting a brick wall. My consistency finally paid off, however. She also needed my help financially. Four to five weeks had gone by, and they moved back home. She brought all our belongings back, as well. I was excited and open to making it work. We were still taking it slow as we slept in separate rooms, but at least they were home.

I must admit I prayed about our relationship, but I didn't wait for direction. I had my mind made up to do what I wanted to do. What I felt was best. Our co-parent journey had begun and since this was new to me, it was different. I was willing to take what I could get, given the circumstances. This process was very rough for me, not only emotionally, but spiritually. In our relationship, she was not trying. She was still clubbing, hanging out, and not coming home. I was at a point where my decisions had to be based on what was best for my kids' future and not on what I wanted. It was time for me to let this relationship go because it was obvious, she already had made up her mind that it would no longer be an "us."

A month later, she moved out again with Isaiah and Monica. She took the same stuff she had at first. By then, our kids were feeling overwhelmed and confused. I was feeling the same. I realized that it was never going to be *happily ever after.* I had to accept that fact and find a way to move forward with my life. That woman had been in and out of my life for fourteen and a half years. No matter what happened, we always came back to each other. But I knew when she left this time, there was no coming back for us: it was finally over. That was the moment I begin to adopt the phrase, "I don't go back; we are exes for a reason."

She moved across town; that made it easier for me to see the kids. We didn't have a set visitation schedule with them; we just called each other when we wanted to see them. Jewan didn't get any better during these times. He was still having a hard time coping with the situation as a preteen. I must admit, I didn't make it any better by ignoring the emotional toil this had on him. As a parent, sometimes we feel we are the only ones experiencing the hurt and forget the children feel it as well, sometimes even more so.

A month passed and it was April 2012. I continued to work and did what I was supposed to do. My cousin Anthony from California moved in with the boys and me. He was a great help to me with the boys while I was working. Eventually, he started working too, and we helped each other. I reassessed my life; I had to find out who I was and what I wanted next. Anthony was tech-savvy and reintroduced me to Facebook. I was reluctant at first because I was a private person. However, he persuaded me. I believe he was trying to help me keep my mind off my other problems.

He created a Facebook page for me in January, but I never

got on it. The site was new to me, and I figured he knew what he was doing. After a while, I decided to give it a try. I started browsing, and as I was browsing, I received a friend request from someone I hadn't spoken with in thirteen years. I knew this person from a trade school. I

My Facebook profile
picture my cousin posted

accepted her friend request. We exchanged phone numbers

because she informed me that she had something important to talk with me about. I had no idea that what she had to tell me would be so important. We talked and she informed me that we had an 11-year-old daughter together. Yes! I was shocked, to say the least. I could not deny my daughter because I knew her mother and I had a past. Immediately, I accepted the role of Katlyn's dad.

My newly found child's mother came into my life when I was young. During that time, my life was unstable, I was living that "street" life. Christy and I were "off" at that point. I was free to date whomever I wanted and vice versa. This young lady was different: she was cool but smart at the same time. She was someone I enjoyed "kicking it" with. Nevertheless, our relationship was short-lived, and we went our separate ways after I graduated from trade school.

I had no idea that what she had to tell me would be so important.

After hearing the life-changing news about my daughter, life for the boys and I still moved forward. During this time, I planned to let the boys finish the school year in Hot Springs, but the next school year, they would move in with my mom and transfer to Warren School District. This also gave us another reason to leave our current apartment, where my neighbor had continued to complain about the noise level. Anthony and I were both working, so that meant the boys were at home by themselves. I would see them throughout the week when I wasn't working, so I felt moving them in with my mom was the best solution as I didn't want my kids to be taken from me.

It had been two weeks since I spoke with my new daughter's mom and the day had come for me to meet her for the first time. I drove up to her house with the boys along. I was nervous and excited at the same time. It hadn't been a struggle for me to tell the boys about their new sister; they were excited as I was. We got out of the car and my daughter, Katlyn, walked up to me. My first impression was she looked just like me. I knew the minute I laid eyes on her that Katlyn was my daughter without a doubt. We hugged and I introduced her to her new brothers. I was hopeful and excited about the journey to come.

Two people on seemingly separate paths faced decisions that changed the course of their journey. Some decisions made seemed small at the moment; however, they eventually had life-changing consequences. What decisions have you made that have changed the trajectory of your life?

Chapter 4

What Season Is This?

Seasons are good to have; they are indications of change on the horizon. There is something new; a fresh start to look forward to. God created winter, spring, summer, and fall as examples that things do come to an end. There are times and seasons for all things. The one thing we love about seasons is that they don't go from one extreme to the next, but the cool winds of fall gradually drop into the cold breeze of winter. Likewise, the warm heat of spring goes into the hotter sunshine of summer. A hot summer night descends from a morning of dew-covered grass to a warm breezy fall afternoon.

LAVONICA'S STORY: Momma improved and was able to leave the rehabilitation center. She was moved to a nursing home about thirty minutes away for long-term care. Dad visited momma faithfully every day, from the time he got off work, staying with her until 10:00 or 11:00 some nights. I didn't go as often as I used to, due to all the chaos at the house. However, Teresa lived in that same town, so she and her family would visit mom regularly. It often made me sad to see momma not able to communicate with us like she used to, but she was strong and kept fighting to get better. I wasn't able to understand everything she tried to say, but I believed in my heart that she understood everything that was going on with us. I quickly realized that she was the glue to our family. The family wasn't the same anymore, especially at the house. While she had been hospitalized, Shun, my niece, had moved out of the house. So, that left Dad; Tywana and her children CJ (15), Ty (14), and Daja (10); and me and my girls. Life didn't stop. We still had to continue to move forward. Tywana and I were both trying our best to deal with the situation, but it was up to us to now juggle the tasks that momma took care of previously. There were many days were cooking, cleaning, homework, trips to practices, and ball games were among those tasks. During that time, delegation wasn't my strongest suit, so if something needed to be done, I would do it myself, mumbling and complaining internally. I tried the best I could to cook, clean, and care for everyone.

My daughter, Lady, didn't make life any better, but who could blame her. Even while I kept parenting Bianca and  Makayla, I had forsaken Lady. I paused being a parent to her. I had so much of my own "crap" going on that I told myself when we move out and get our own place, I would start back giving Lady bedtimes, phone

Stephanie ("Lady"), Bianca, and Makayla

usage restrictions, and more monitoring. Basically, start back parenting her. See, she slept on the living room floor with Tywana's kids, so I allowed her to do whatever she wanted without many restrictions, which was not my character at all.

But during this time, Lady started being defiant toward me. She would get a very bad attitude with me. She wouldn't come home after cheering at games. The communication we once had was gone, and I was informed that she began spending time with boys without me knowing. My innocent little girl had disappeared right before my blinded eyes.

I remember one specific incident when Ty came home after the game, but Lady wasn't with her. I asked Ty, "Where is Lady?" She said, "Lady said she was going to get something to eat at McDonald's." Lady did not call for permission or anything. I politely got in my minivan with my robe, house shoes, and bonnet on my head, and I drove to McDonald's. Teenagers were everywhere. I got out of my van with no shame and walked into McDonald's asking everyone if they had seen Lady. Everyone that I asked told me no. I saw one of the guys who went to church with. I asked him, and he acted like he didn't know me. Dressed like I was, I couldn't really blame him. Finally, I walked out the door, and there she was, with a boy! I grabbed her and yanked her into the vehicle. She

Stephanie "Lady" and Tycoriana "Ty"

asked me if I went into McDonald's dressed like I was, and with a grin on my face, I replied, "I sure did." She started crying and sobbing. She was so embarrassed. I thought to myself, "I bet she will never play this stunt again." I must say, she never did. However, her attitude didn't get any better. One day, Daddy ended up having to discipline her for being so disrespectful to me.

On top of that, my long-distance relationship with Chris was getting complicated. He moved to Texas to get out of Los Angeles. Even though he moved closer, it was still a long-distance relationship. Our conversations at times felt strained due to my relationship with God and my knowledge of him not having a relationship with God. Nor was he serious about trying to get one. Some days we talked for hours and some days he would be talking out of his head. He didn't have any children of his own, but I would still share all my kids' stories and problems with him. Even over the phone, it was like he really didn't care too much for my kids, or maybe, he just didn't know much about parenting.

He would always suggest the choice of whopping or grounding them for everything. Despite it all, I felt compelled to teach him how a parent should parent, and I continued to daydream of the day we would say "I do."

The holidays were approaching quickly; it was getting closer to Thanksgiving. Fred had gotten in touch and wanted to see the girls and me. After much pleading and begging, I finally gave in and said yes. I never wanted to be the woman that kept a dad from his children. My mind was already made up that nothing was moving forward with us, anyway. I was excited that Makayla would get a chance to see her dad because it had been a while. Fred made his arrival and for the first time in twelve years, I wasn't obligated to him. It felt good knowing I didn't owe him any apologies, any excuses, or anything at all. Without ever confessing it, I felt he knew I was right for leaving. Now, it probably wasn't right how I left, but the reasons for leaving were justified.

We went to the nursing home for him to speak to Momma. I don't remember whose idea it was, but it wasn't a good one. Momma had a confused look on her face looking at him. It was like I felt in my spirit that she was saying, "Nooooo, Vonna! I know you are not back with him." I reassured her that he was just visiting for the holiday. I can truly say that I was glad to see that Thanksgiving come and go and that season was ending. I waved goodbye to Fred, and he went back on his way to Baton Rouge.

◆ ◆ ◆

TIM'S STORY: The boys were all settled in Warren and had no problems at all. I talked with them every day and tried my best to see them at least three times a week. I believe this move was good for them because they were able to get that motherly care from my mom. I continued to work, save money, and stay focused. One of my older cousins pastored a church in Malvern,

I kept my mind on God because I knew He would be the one to help me through this.

so Anthony and I started attending regularly. He gave me a few opportunities to minister as well. That was something I enjoyed doing. I kept my mind on God because I knew He would be the one to help me through this.

Thanksgiving was coming up and the months passed quickly for me. I knew my lease on my apartment was ending, and I needed to be prepared to make my next move. During that season in my life, God gave me peace, and I was truly thankful.

It is amazing how seconds make minutes, minutes make hours, hours make days, days make months, and months make years. So that means, even what we do with a second of time... matters. We don't have time to live in regret and replay mistakes. We all must live, learn, and move forward. The seasons are designed to bring change and one must change with it. If not, it is like wearing a coat in the summer and flip-flops in the winter.

Chapter 5

Catching Up with the Past

Google defines the word "past" as gone by in time and no longer existing. How can a person catch up with something that no longer exists? It's called memories. Whether there are good or bad memories from the past, making peace, has to be a part of the process to move forward. Peace to move on is sometimes taken for granted. It is not given to everyone in every situation. However, when it is given, it is best to give God the glory because no one but Him blessed you with it. There is nothing like waking up in the morning and feeling hopeful about the future, despite the past; knowing everything is going to work out for the good. That is our personal definition of peace.

LAVONICA'S STORY: I invited Chris down to visit for the holiday. He gladly accepted the invitation, and we made arrangements for him to stay with Teresa and Corey. I wouldn't have ever met Chris if it wasn't for Teresa.

Chris was Teresa's best friend in college. It was 1995. Teresa brought Chris home with her one day and Chris liked what he saw: me. I was beautiful, vibrant, and full of life. I was also a junior in high school. It wasn't long before we started dating and became inseparable. Despite him attending college forty-five minutes away, Chris would come to visit me five to six days out of the week. Our relationship was intense, and he would tell me often how in love he was with me.

I found out that I was pregnant by him in January 1996. I was sad, and Chris wasn't happy about it either. The next thing I knew, we were talking about abortion. That was something that I never thought I would ever do, however, my opinion at that time didn't really matter. It was February 21, 1996, and we were on our way to Little Rock to end a life before it really got started. No one knew I went through a period of depression because of that process. A month or two later, I finally came out of the depression. Our relationship shifted, and things weren't quite the same.

In May 1996, I graduated from high school. Chris decided to finish his college education in California and moved back home to Los Angeles after the spring semester of the same year. Our plan was for me to move to Torrance, California with my uncle and attend college, which would make me closer to him. We would graduate college, get married, and live happily ever after.

I moved to California in the Fall of 1996. I hadn't been in California long before I got homesick and wanted to see my family. I got a round-trip ticket to go home for Christmas and return to California after the new year.

I enjoyed being with my family for Christmas. However, on New Year's Eve, I received a phone call from my former pastor's wife, First Lady Hazel Washington. She wanted to meet at the church at 9:00 a.m. She invited Patrick, Sis Patterson (Patrick's mom), Stacy (her daughter), and me. When we got there, she gave us a word she received from the Lord. She said it was a "Do or Die" deal for us. She told us about our deaths in detail down to the color of our caskets. It was that God had a special calling on our lives and we had to give Him our lives. Consequently, on December 31, 1996, I gave God my life that morning; all of us did. Sister Patterson rededicated her life to God. However, my prophecy went a little farther: I was told that I wasn't able to go back to California. I was devastated, hurt, and confused. I called

Chris to share with him the good and bad news. The good news was that I had gotten saved and dedicated my life to God, but the bad news was I wasn't going back to California. He was devastated as well. We cried and talked all night on the phone. By the end of the conversation, he said he was coming to get me and take me back to California. He kept his word and came to get me, but I was too scared to go. So, he went back to California without me.

Chris and I decided we were going to still make it work by having a long-distance relationship. We talked on the phone every day. We talked a lot about our future together and still planned to get married one day. I cried many of days and asked God, "Why?" I couldn't seem to grasp what was going on. I would talk with Chris about him giving his life to God. He responded by telling me, he will at his own time. He didn't want me to pressure him. He would say, he always pictured us giving our lives to God at the same time. It wasn't fair for me to make that decision without him.

A month passed, and I tried my best to live a saved, sanctified life. It was not easy for me. My life, my plans were all messed up. What came next changed the whole trajectory of my life. A guy named Perry from Omaha came to Hope to visit his family. I had known him since we were kids. We would talk every once in a while. However, this time he wanted to visit me, and one thing led to another. I knew I had gotten pregnant that night by a person I wasn't in love with. The months passed, and I felt my life was spinning out of control. I wasn't only confessing to still being saved, but I had a whole baby in my belly, hiding it.

No one in my family knew about Perry. I was in distress to confess my sin; that I was pregnant, and the baby father's was not Chris. My stomach had grown by the weeks. My sleep and eating habits had also changed. In the meantime, Chris had proposed to me over the phone, and I said yes. He mailed the engagement ring to me. I was in a state of delusion and confusion. Mentally, I wasn't stable and wasn't making good decisions at all.

Four months later, I confessed to Chris that I was pregnant with Perry's child, and no one knew about it. Chris was so in love with me that he suggested that we not tell anyone that the baby belonged to someone else. Chris would claim the baby as his own, but under one condition: "That nigga don't come to our doorstep." My response was, "I know he wants to be a part of his child's life." He said, "Well I see who you want to be with." Which eventually led to a tragic ending to our future together. It's sad to say, but Perry wasn't a part of this child's life much at all. And even sadder, I found out he was married, and his wife was one month pregnant behind me.

The past was the past, and I had made peace with it. It was the Christmas season and joy was all in the atmosphere. It had been fifteen years since I saw Chris, I could not believe that moment was

> *I truly understand what it means to make peace with the past in order to move forward in forgiveness.*

believe that moment was happening again. I couldn't believe that fate had brought us back together. My family was so happy to see him, to see us back together again. It didn't take long before Chris and Teresa got back acquainted. They were acting as they did in college. It felt good to see them so happy together, reminiscing about old times.

After the hugs, smiles, and catching up, Chris and I had the hard conversation of "why" I did what I did. However, I wasn't ever going to be able to give a good answer for why. All I could think of was that I was selfish and immature. There wasn't any answer that could or would justify cheating on a person I said that I loved. There was no way that I could change the decision I made at that time. If I could, I would have; but as stated before, the past was the past. I could still sense some bitterness, however, despite apologizing a thousand times. Further, one of the hardest conversations Chris and I had was about the decision we made in February of 1996. It was a decision that changed our lives forever. It had taken God's power, grace, and mercy to help me get over that unforgiveness, guilt, and shame that I had to carry for many, many years for not carrying my child. I truly understand what it means to make peace with the past in order to move forward in forgiveness.

The saddest part is that he never had any kids. He said that particular pregnancy was his only opportunity, and he regretted the abortion. He finally came clean with me and told me the truth. He said that he told his mom I was pregnant, and she forced him to have it done. All we had, at this point, was the hope of putting the past behind us and moving forward to see if it would work this time.

Christmas day came; and with it, came a reality check. Chris shared with me that he suffered from rheumatoid arthritis, but I didn't know how severe it was until that night. He had left his medication, and he had a flare-up. I ended up taking him to the emergency room that night. Teresa said that was God's way of showing me the truth. I remembered my dad even commented, which was out of his character. He tried to help me think about how the future would look with the additional responsibility of caring for an adult in addition to my children.

Not only was he dealing with RA, Chris wanted me to take him to the liquor store. He said it helped ease the pain. "Was he crazy?" That is exactly what I asked him! He was even smoking. "Jeez," I thought! "What have I gotten myself *What have I gotten myself into?* into?" My guilt kept me rationalizing this craziness. I felt I owed it to him to stay, and I was determined to be there for him showing him I had his back.

I did not want to judge him or leave him. I was determined to make our relationship work. I said to myself that God could save him and change him. So, after the holiday passed, we decided to recommit to each other and begin to plan a future together. In the meantime, Teresa demanded that I break up with him, for she saw right through him.

♦ ♦ ♦

TIM'S STORY: All my Christmas shopping was finished, and I knew the kids would be happy with the gifts I purchased for them. This was my first Christmas being a single dad. It was one of my best Christmases because I had all my children. Katlyn's mom even let Katlyn's sister come over for Christmas. We all spent time together in Warren at my mom's house. It didn't take long before everyone got acquainted with each other. It's like

Katlyn had been with us her entire life. She and her sister fit right in. During this time, I didn't think about what was next: I enjoyed the moment and memories with family. Mom was excited, to say the least. Not only was Christmas her favorite holiday, but to see all her grandbabies together was a dream come true.

My mom, Marion, was a great support to me. She continued to encourage me to be a great dad and stay with the Lord. She

mastered the word "servanthood." She was and is the epitome of a caretaker. She was caring for my uncle and auntie during this time. On top of that, she welcomed in my kids, all in the name of supporting and helping me. She always made the Christmas season special because ever since she had grandbabies,

L-R Top: Katlyn's sister, Katlyn, Jewan, Danovan (Jewan's friend), Bottom: Isaiah, Ahmod, and Monica

she spoiled them rotten. She would buy more gifts for them than for me.

Mom didn't treat Katlyn or her sister any differently, she had plenty of gifts for both of them. I remembered when I first told mom about Katlyn and how I found out that I had an 11-year-old daughter. I called her the same day that I found out. We were both in shock. Mom was ready to meet her that day. She started asking me when I was going to bring her down to meet her. I had to remind her that I hadn't met her yet. At Christmas, I finally had an opportunity to have Katlyn meet mom. Mom said she looked exactly like me. She ran into the house and got my baby picture to prove it. I believe Katlyn fell in love with my mom, just like all the other

L-R Top: Jewan, Tim, Katlyn, Isaiah, Bottom: Ahmod and Monica

grandkids did. Mom kept saying she wished Grandma Sue Ella could have met her, she knew they would have loved each other. Katlyn is my child: we had a pizza-eating contest; which, unfortunately, she did not win. However, she was not ashamed to eat, or be competitive, and that's my type of girl.

The holiday had ended, and the time came to get back to the real world. I knew eventually that Katlyn and I were going to have a real conversation about me just now coming into her life. I felt I would not initiate that conversation. I would let her ask in her timing. We said our goodbyes and her mom picked the two girls up from Warren.

The new year brought in a year of reflection for me. The reality was that I was a divorced, single dad of five. I had 30 days until my lease would end on my apartment, and I would have to move back to Warren with my mom. That being said, I would have to commute from Warren to Hot Springs to work. I have no desire to stay in Warren permanently. Eventually, I would get us moved back to Hot Springs. Christy and I didn't communicate as we should have, but it was decent. The only obligation I had was to Katlyn, to make up for the lost time by spending as much time as possible with her.

A month passed, and Anthony got his own apartment in Hot Springs. I ended up moving back with my mom in Warren. I would spend some nights over at Anthony's when I had to work back-to-back days. During that time, it seemed to make sense to just quit my job and get one in Warren. However, I liked my job. I felt I was making a difference in the world helping at-risk youth every day. The reason I was so passionate about my job was because I had been an at-risk youth myself. I didn't have a father figure growing up, so that left me doing and learning a lot of things on my own, even if that meant the hard way. My mom and Grandma Sue Ella did the best they could to help me.

On the ride up there, I had made up in my mind that I was not staying.

A MESSAGE NOTIFICATION

It was 1996, and I was fifteen years old when mom and Aunt Vicki dropped me off in Little Rock at Camp Robinson Youth Challenge Program. It was a court order due to my defiant behavior. On the ride up there, I had made up my mind that I was not staying. I went AWOL that same night. I ended up getting caught and went to jail. Needless to say, I had to go back to Camp Robinson. I eventually saw that it was a successful program: it made me realize I had a lot of growing up to do. It made me into a man; made me grow up using discipline and structure. Those defining moments put a burning in me that programs like Camp Robinson do work. However, it takes passionate workers and mentors to help those types of youth. That is the example I was determined to be for the at-risk youth at Ouachita Children's Center.

There is no doubt in our minds that our past played a big role in our lives. However, there is a very thin line between letting it define us versus confine us. Sometimes we allow the past good times to confine us and keep us stuck. The polar opposite is allowing the past to define you...to explain or clarify why you like you are.

Chapter 6

What Has My Thinking Gotten Me Into?

According to Google, we have 6,000 thoughts per day. The Bible tells us, "As a man thinketh in his heart, so is he." There is a multitude of videos, articles, books, and quotes about guarding the way we think. Trust us: your body will take you to the places you thought about the most, not the other way around. If you want something different, the first step is simple…think about it!

LAVONICA'S STORY: Chris and I decided we were going to make our relationship work despite all the hurdles. However, deep down inside, I knew I was trying too hard to make this work due to guilt and trying to be more loyal this time around. I was confused during this season in my life. I was really in conflict due to my relationship with God and how that impacted my relationship with Chris. I knew that he wasn't a true, God-fearing man. He wasn't the type of man that would pray for me, or that would pray together with me. I thought maybe one day I could change him. Maybe I was put into his life to help him with his relationship with God. Occasionally, I would be real with myself and think, "I jumped from the frying pan to the skillet," meaning from Fred to Chris, there wasn't much of a difference.

It was February 24, 2013. After church that Sunday afternoon, I checked my Facebook page, which had become custom. I had a message notification time-stamped February 24, 2013, at 12:19 from a guy named Timothy Davis that said, "Hey!" I asked my sister, Tywana, if she knew him because they were friends on Facebook. She said that she didn't know him at all. Then, I went to his profile page to see if I should have known him, but I still couldn't recall knowing him. I immediately replied to him and said, "Hey...do I suppose to know you?" Tim let me know that I didn't know him, and he didn't know me, he just liked my pictures on Facebook. I thought that was very strange, and I never told Chris about it either.

Three days straight, I got message notifications from Tim. The messages started, "Hello friend" and "Hello, how are you?" He also gave me his phone number and requested that I texted him. I intentionally ignored the messages because I was trying to be loyal to Chris. I just wasn't interested in getting to know someone else. It was March 1st, and he messaged me again asking about my day and if I would text him. That time, I politely replied and asked him about his day, but I completely ignored that part about texting him. He wasn't going to have my personal contact information. Tim continued to message me a few times the next week. Once again, I didn't respond. I had other things on my mind, and a relationship – or even friendship – with Tim was the last thing I thought I needed. I knew that I was in some kind of relationship with Chris. What kind? I wasn't sure, but I just didn't need any more distractions in my life right then. Tim refused to take no for an answer, however. He became politely persistent, if that is such a thing.

> *I immediately replied back to him and said, "Hey...do I suppose to know you?*

A MESSAGE NOTIFICATION

I went to church on Sunday, March 10th, and I received a word from God through one of the preachers, Elder Lee Artis Burton, Jr. He told me, "God is about to make you happy, and you're about to do something that everybody won't understand." I came up with my conclusion about what I thought was meant by that prophesy. I thought it was about my plan to move to Dallas with Chris and start a new life together. I was preparing myself mentally that everyone wasn't going to understand that I had planned to get married again so soon. I got home from church and did my usual routine: cooking, eating, and relaxing. Once again, when I checked my Facebook, I had a message notification from Tim with a message about exchanging numbers. He, once again, asked how my day had been. It had been a while since I responded to his last message. So, I decided to reply, but quickly changed my mind and texted him instead.

I shared with Tim my plans to move to Dallas. We began to have a personal dialogue about each other lives. I learned that Tim was also recently divorced and had five children – two of whom lived with him in a town that was only an hour and a half away. He loved God just as much as I did, and we were members of the same denomination, the Church of God in Christ. He shared with me his love for basketball and his love of travel. I told myself that this is wrong, snapped out of it, and ended the text conversation. The next morning, Tim texted me, "Good morning, I pray you to have a good day."

We found ourselves texting each other throughout the day. Day after day, his good morning text became routine, and it was something I looked forward to. We began to form a real friendship in a short amount of time. In this friendship, we realized quickly that we had a strong and similar emotional and spiritual bond.

♦ ♦ ♦

TIM'S STORY: I was tired of being single and felt it was time for me to try this love thing again. I decided to go on a few dates; however, didn't much come out of it at all. I realized that my standards had changed. I understood what I didn't want more clearly than I understood what I did want. Additionally, I was in no hurry to rush into a relationship. However, I knew I wanted to be married again one day. I always liked the feeling of having a partner in life, a teammate. The fact that I belonged to someone and she belonged to me made me feel good. Someone to hold me accountable and we simply do life

> *I decided to give dating a break and focus on my job and children.*

together. How quickly I discovered that some women my age didn't have this type of mindset. The few I dated, God was not number one in their life, so having a positive, promising future wasn't on their agenda. It was all about drinking, smoking, and clubbing on the weekends; just "kicking it" in other words.

I decided to give dating a break and focus on my job and children. During this time, I stayed occupied to keep my mind off my singleness. Being single was a difficult time for me because I was used to being in a relationship. I knew this was new territory I was emerging into, and it wasn't easy. Being saved and a single parent left me with limited options on what I exposed my children and myself to. I had a no-compromise, no-nonsense mindset. I would go to church and see couples, and I desired that for myself. My hope was, in due time, it would come to pass. I knew I loved God, and I wanted a wife that would be the same way. So, I was willing to wait for the latter.

I can remember vividly the day I got a friend request on Facebook from a guy I attended job corps with when I was in Little Rock. Immediately, I accepted his friend request. Because of this, Facebook suggested I became friends with a lady named Tywana Tidwell, whom I did not know. I accepted the suggestion and sent her a friend request because of her profile picture. She had a family picture with her siblings, dad, and mom. I was attracted to the woman in the gray shirt. She looked

so beautiful to me. Also, I knew her dad from being a part of the Arkansas 3rd Jurisdiction Church of God In Christ. So, with that being said, I knew she had a good upbringing and that she knew something about the Lord.

Tywana's Facebook Profile Picture: L-R Front: Kenneth, Gladys, L-R Back: Teresa, Christi, Kelvin, Tywana, and Lavonica

I began to look for her on Facebook by searching through Tywana's friend list. I found her, and I was so excited! Her name was Lavonica Watson. I got the courage to step out on faith because I was a little nervous. I didn't know if she was married or anything; I didn't know anything about her. I Facebook messaged her and said, "Hey!" She messaged me back and said, "Hey...do I suppose to know you?" I told her she didn't know me, and I didn't know her. However, I knew her dad. She didn't type anything after that. I thought maybe she was not interested.

I tried not to be overbearing, but I kept thinking about her. Meanwhile, I would check out her Facebook page and look at her pictures. I decided to reach out again and asked how her day was going. However, I got no response. I reached out to her a couple of more times throughout the week, and again, no response. I begin to think maybe she was not into me. I wanted to pursue this woman, but I didn't want to give the impression of being desperate. I tried to be smooth with it. However, another part of me was proceeding with caution because it was social media. I kept looking at all her pictures to make sure she wasn't catfishing me. I had a lot of mixed feelings. "Maybe she might be the one," was one of the thoughts that I had. I also had thoughts on whether I should move on, what my next move should be, or whether I should make no move at all.

I talked myself into trying one more time to reach out to her. I was in a dilemma with trying to show her that I was very interested, but at the same time not displaying characteristics of a stalker. I finally did it: I messaged her on Facebook again and asked her about her day. I also gave her my number again so she could text me. She finally responded and asked me about my day. I saw this little crack in the door and walked right in. I began to Facebook message her daily. However, during this whole time, the Facebook messaging situation was a little inconvenient for me because I had poor internet service where I was staying. I was going to a local restaurant using their Wi-Fi. So, if or when she responded, I would drive to the restaurant for Wi-Fi service to message her back. I kept giving her my number and asking if we could text, but she would not text me. Of course, I didn't tell her the reason why, but it didn't stop me from asking. On Sunday, March 10th, I guess the Lord touched her heart or something. I checked on her, and instead of getting the usual Facebook message reply, she texted me! Now, we were making some progress! That day, we were finally able to have a real conversation via text. I found out a lot of details about her, and I was able to share information with her about me. However, with all that was said, she informed me that she was planning to move to Dallas. At that moment, I felt that I had wasted my time, but I had two options. Option one would allow her to go

Now we were making progress! ahead and move on, or option two, give her a reason to change her mind and stay. I chose option two. I knew I was going to do everything in my power to give her a reason to stay.

I could no longer keep this to myself. I decided to share with my mom and my cousin Anthony what was going on with the young lady that I had started pursuing. They were happy for me. They knew I was very interested in her because if I wasn't, I would have never mentioned her to them. I knew I was on borrowed time before her move to Dallas, so I began texting her every day throughout the day. The best part about this was that it wasn't one-sided. We were texting each other throughout the day. We were becoming really good friends. Things were moving pretty fast, and I was just enjoying the ride. All I knew was there was something special about this woman and something even more special about the thought of us.

We cannot blame anyone but ourselves for where we are in our lives. Our thoughts got us there. Many people have a bad habit of blaming others, the past, and even bad circumstances for their current unhappiness. However, it is just best to go look in the mirror if you are feeling sorry for yourself or having a pity party. What you will see is your reflection looking back at you. The only way to get on "Change Avenue" is to think yourself on it. Change your thoughts, change your life!

Chapter 7

Never Have I Ever

The phrase, Never Have I Ever, is considered a present perfect tense statement. Meaning, it is used to show an action that happened in the past that is directly related to the present. A great example of this is what Jesus did on the cross more than two thousand years ago. John 3:16 (KJV) states, "For God so loved the world, that he gave his only begotten Son, that whosoever believeth in him should not perish, but have everlasting life." He has shed his blood for us to have the right relationship with God. Never have I ever seen a love so demonstrated. Through this, we have experienced some "never have I ever" moments.

LAVONICA'S STORY: It was a normal Thursday in March. As was my routine, I went to work. I looked at my phone in expectation of a good morning text from Tim, but my phone was dead. I found myself at work praying to God because I was in conflict about my relationship with Chris and my friendship with Tim. It had become apparent to me that my friendship with Tim was

I was tired of struggling for something that wasn't meant to be.

much better than my relationship with Chris. I was holding onto Chris for what we had in the past and not what it was in that moment. I remember every detail about this moment. I was standing on the assembly line facing the east wall. At that moment, I was tired; tired of myself and tired of fighting for what I thought was best for me. I was tired of struggling for something that wasn't meant to be. At that moment, I surrendered to God. I surrendered every part of my being to God. I told God, "Let your will be done in my life!" I meant it, too; no one around to impress, just God and me, at that moment. I will never forget what happened next.

God spoke to my spirit, not out loud, but in my innermost soul, and said, "You're about to miss out on something great...Tim that is." I believe God said Tim's name specifically, so I wouldn't be confused. The very next thought I had was that

I was done with Chris, and I was going to end our relationship when I got home that day. Then I said a prayer to God and said, "If Tim is the man for me, let him call me today!" Mind you, we had only been texting each other up until this point. The crazy part about the request that I made is that I forgot my phone was dead. I asked everyone I knew, who normally had their charger with them, if I could borrow theirs. Every one of them said they didn't bring it to work that day. However, I didn't change the request I made to God. So, when I got home, I put my phone on the charger and did exactly what I had said. I called Chris and told him that our relationship was over. At first, he got upset. Then, he said he understood. I was at peace with that decision and felt relieved.

Hours passed and no text or call from Tim. I began to accept the fact that Tim was probably not the one God designed for me. I was due to be at church in an hour; Mother Early was conducting a revival at our church. I started getting ready while checking my phone every two minutes. Thirty minutes later, I got a text from Tim asking if he could call me. Immediately, with shaking hands, I texted back "Yes!" I finally heard his voice for the first time. I felt like a little teenage girl again. Of course, I made sure he was not aware of my excitement. He politely spoke and asked about my day, and then he went into telling me a story I would never forget.

◆ ◆ ◆

TIM'S STORY: I was so excited about starting a new journey with someone who I was very interested in getting to know. I must admit that I was a little nervous because I had never felt this way before. That was what led me to stop and pray. That is something I always do when I don't know what to do. I prayed and asked God for a sign. I asked God that if this was the woman for me, then when I text her and ask permission to call her, she would say yes. If she agreed to the call, I would tell her that I was an Elder of a church and planned to be a pastor one day. If she supported that, then I would know, for sure, she was the woman for me.

Time passed and it was around 6 p.m. I texted her and asked if I could call her, and she agreed to the call. I heard her voice for the first time. I was so nervous, too. The sign was revealed, and I knew without a doubt this woman was meant to be in my life. I knew I wanted a wife, but I knew there was a process. I felt awkward and ashamed at first, but I told her anyway. I told her that I prayed for her and asked

God orchestrated and set His approval on our relationship.

God for a sign. The sign was, if she was the woman for me, she would answer when I called her today. Once I told her that, I was relieved. I must say, I was very honest and transparent. In response, she told me something that I knew only God could do! She said she prayed for me today also asking God for a sign. She told me her sign was that if I was the man for her, God, "let him call me today." We were both blown away by how God orchestrated and set His approval on our relationship. I was also relieved with her accepting me as an ordained Elder. I told her about my calling, and she was okay with it. I breathed a sigh of relief knowing, without a doubt, I was finally headed in the right direction with my life. We give all honor and glory to God!

♦ ♦ ♦ OUR STORY – INTERWINED ♦ ♦ ♦

LAVONICA: After I got home from church, Tim and I talked some more over the phone. We talked all night long actually. It seemed that we had known each other for years. "Wow!" is how we both felt. This wasn't just a coincidence! We finally felt that we had met the person we were supposed to be with.

On March 16, 2013 (it was a Saturday morning), Tim called and let me know that he wanted to meet me face-to-face. Makayla had just finished making me breakfast in bed. She made me a peanut butter, jelly, and tuna fish sandwich. I wasn't sure if this was a foreseen sign that something unusual was about to take place or a setup for "bubble guts" to get me out of the date. Either way, I was thankful for Makayla's effort, and pretended to eat was she prepared. I informed Tim that I had a church engagement out of town. I couldn't meet that day, but I told him that I would work something out. I didn't plan to meet him face to face so soon. I was caught off guard by his request. However, I went along with it anyway. We decided on a time and a place. He decided to take me to Bossier City, Louisiana, for our first date.

Immediately, I got up and made adjustments for the event I was scheduled to attend. I also made arrangements with a babysitter for Bianca and Makayla. Lady had prior plans to spend the night at her friend's house, so she was taken care of. I started searching for the best outfit to wear. Honestly, in this part, I was the most nervous. I wanted to impress him. You'd think I'd be anxious about going out with somebody I didn't know, but I wasn't uneasy about it at all. I finally selected my outfit and got all "dolled up." The clock was ticking, and the time was drawing near to meet the man who made my heart beat a hundred times a minute. I couldn't be still; I was going from room to room. Finally, he called to let me know that he was outside. I didn't have to worry about formalities with introducing him to anyone because Tywana and I were the only ones at the house that day

and she was asleep. As he knocked on the door, my heart began pounding and my hands were sweating as I walked over to the door to open it. My thought when I first laid eyes on him was how much younger

Lavonica and Tim's
First Date in Bossier City, LA
(first picture together)

than me he looked. Even though he was three years younger, it seemed like it was more than that. I remember exactly what he had on: a black collared church shirt with gray on the collar and black dress pants. My second thought was, "this man looks really good: tall, mocha, and handsome...my, my, my!" We greeted each other, introduced ourselves, and hugged. At that moment it seemed that time stood still just for us. Goosebumps covered my body, and I felt a sense of relief and excitement at the same time. He asked if I was ready to go and I said yes. I grabbed my purse, and we got in his car and headed to Bossier City, LA.

◆ ◆ ◆

TIM: The reason I called Lavonica on that Saturday was that I was excited; I was ready to move forward. I wanted to see what she looked like in person. I was so glad when she agreed.

A MESSAGE NOTIFICATION

When we met, I had just left a youth service in Pine Bluff, Arkansas; and I still had my church clothes on. During the entire drive to Hope, I was thinking of different things that we could do in Bossier City to make this date memorable for us. As I drove up to her house, I didn't waste any time calling to let her know that I was outside. She met me at the door. She was so beautiful with such a beautiful smile. Honestly, I was relieved that she looked exactly like her pictures on Facebook.

We were on our way to Bossier City to the Boardwalk. The conversation on the way was not forced, nor was it awkward. We talked about a lot of different things. Everything just flowed well. I enjoyed having so much to talk about with Lavonica. Despite us being around so many other people, it felt like we were the only ones around. I was living in the moment.

While eating, we had a deep discussion about marriage, including what we desired from a marriage. Time wasn't a factor. I was captivated by the moment, not realizing that I had to be at work in Hot Spring, Arkansas, at 6 o'clock the next morning, and we were still at the restaurant when midnight arrived.

◆ ◆ ◆

LAVONICA: Not only did we stroll the Boardwalk having great conversation, we held hands the entire time too. It was so beautiful and memorable that we decided to take a selfie to capture the moment. I did not have a care in the world, nor did I care what others were thinking of us. My focus was on Tim. He had my undivided attention.

We started getting hungry, but by that time it was late. Most of the restaurants on the Boardwalk were closed. The only restaurant that was still open and that we agreed on was IHOP. We were seated and began having serious conversation; conversation that stemmed around real-life stuff. His relationship with God, his children, and the fact that he knew exactly what he wanted in life were the three things that touched my heart. That night, all the different weights that I had been carrying, my past hurts, my divorce from Fred, my bad choices... all were released from me. Tim made me feel secure and hopeful of a great future on the horizon.

There was something supernatural taking place. Still to this day, it is hard to put words to it. All I knew was my heart had connected with him on another level. I was trying my best to suppress those feelings. I even questioned myself wondering how I could have such deep feelings for this man whom I barely knew. I mean it was instant love! It was late and we decided that it was time to go. We still had a long ride back to Hope.

We had just made it to Hope, Arkansas, and while talking, something slipped out of my mouth. I did not plan it, but I told him that I loved him. I had no intention of saying those three words to him that night. The Bible says, Matthew 12:34b (CEB), ".....What fills the heart comes out of the mouth." It came from my heart, and my mouth could not help but speak it.

♦ ♦ ♦

TIM: Yeah, she did! I was happy about it. I did not hesitate to reply that I loved her too. However, I must admit that I was surprised. It wasn't because I was an unlovable guy, but because I felt the same way about her. I was just too nervous to say it. I didn't want to scare her or make her feel uncomfortable. Once I saw that our feelings were mutual, I gladly replied, "I love you too."

That was the moment that our lives shifted. I became exposed to true love. We were no longer "twain," but we became one that night: mentally, spiritually, and emotionally connected. It had gotten serious; it was no room for games. My thought was, "It's up from here!"

From that moment on, we decided to be together, to be a couple. I got her back home safely, and I was waiting on a kiss. However, she stopped me saying she wanted to save our first kiss for our wedding day. This woman was full of surprises! But, I liked it. I agreed to that, and we both knew that marriage was in our future. From that day forward, we were inseparable; either texting, talking, or together.

♦ ♦ ♦

LAVONICA: The Lord had put it on my heart to save our first kiss for our wedding day. Initially, I wanted to ignore this small, yet big instruction. However, it was so heavy on my heart, that I could not ignore it. I told Tim and he seemed slightly disappointed, but quickly obliged my request. We ended that perfect night with a hug.

I woke up the next morning, and what could have been a typical Sunday morning for most people, was a new beginning for me. My world had been turned right side up. I was filled with so many good emotions. I went to church and couldn't wait to get home to tell Tywana all about my time with Tim. She was happy for me. While she was a little cautious and concerned for me, overall she was happy and believed that this was God's doing. After church, I reminisced on the entire date with Tim. I still had "butterflies" in my stomach. It was amazing how all the hurt and pain that I experienced in the past was eradicated. I no longer felt sorry for myself. I had awakened to love and was hopeful about my future with Tim.

The flashback of me telling him that I loved him the night before replayed in my mind several times. The feeling of embarrassment and regret tried to creep into my mind. "Was his response *It was amazing how all the hurt and pain that I experienced in the past was eradicated.* out of courtesy when he said, 'I love you too', or was it genuine… did he feel what I felt," was the question that I kept pondering. I stopped trying to rationalize it and accepted the truth; I loved him. The love that I felt wasn't all eros (sexual), but pure, innocent, God-given love. It was a feeling that I never felt for any man.

◆ ◆ ◆

TIM: I made it back to Hot Springs at 4 am after my first date with someone I already caught feelings for. Getting in at this time made 6 a.m. an incredibly early morning for me. All the way home that night, however, I kept questioning if there it was possible to feel true love after one date. All day at work the next day, love covered my tiredness. Meaning that I was thinking about Lavonica most of the day. I was thinking about marriage with this woman, where we would live, and just thoughts of being with her daily. Never had I experienced this with any woman. I was wondering if she felt the same about me as I felt about her after just one date.

I couldn't wait to share this with someone. I told my mom and my cousin, Anthony, that I could see myself spending the rest of my life with this woman. It was something about her personality that kindled my love for her.

Being able to experience things you have never experienced takes a certain amount of faith. It takes letting go and trusting that the outcome will work out in your favor. We had the opportunity to encounter some "never have I ever" opportunities. We are glad that we didn't allow our past, our fear, or our doubt to dictate our decision-making on the journey. There are some incidents where you will only find God in the "I give up on MY plans". The Bible states in Jeremiah 29:11 (NLT), "For I know the plans I have for you, says the LORD. They are plans for good and not for disaster, to give you a future and a hope." We said, let go and let God!

Chapter 8

Moments to Tell

The moments that signify change are forever ingrained in your mind. Those are first kisses, wedding proposals and wedding days, childbirths, and words from God. Those moments can be retold with great details. Also, not just a story, but the feelings that supported these stories. Reliving these moments can easily change your mood. So, we would say, when these moments are occurring, enjoy and take note, because trust us, these are stories that will be retold, over and over.

LAVONICA: I couldn't wait to tell my carpool buddies, Kay Kay and Piper about the amazing date that I had with Tim. I knew they would be so happy for me. I was so happy, I had a grin on my face as big as the size of Texas. I was on cloud nine, and my time at work seemed to pass quickly because I talked with Tim on all of my breaks.

I eagerly waited for him to set the pace for our new relationship. Of course, the good morning texts didn't stop, however, some days I got a good morning call. Due to the distance and our conflicting job schedules, we just talked on the phone for the remainder of that week. Lady enjoyed making fun of me saying she could hear me on the phone all night talking and laughing with someone. I couldn't argue with her because that's exactly what we did. We talked about ourselves and life, however, we also loved talking about God and the Bible. We made it a habit to

> *I eagerly waited for him to set the pace for our new relationship.*

pray each night before we got off the phone. We talked for hours until I had to go to work. I was sleep deprived, purely functioning on love.

The weekend was approaching, and we decided it was time to take things a little further. It was time for us to meet each other's children. During this time, I had Stephanie, Bianca, and

Makayla. Tim had Jewan and Ahmod. We chose to have a picnic at the park in Warren.

◆ ◆ ◆

TIM: We felt a picnic at the park would be the best environment for the next step in our relationship to take place. We discussed what we wanted to eat and decided that we both would contribute.

I had to sit the boys down to let them know what was going on. I had been very protective over them, especially when it came to meeting a woman in my life. Since their mom, they had not seen me with another woman. I was in no way dreadful about having the conversation with them, I was happy and excited to tell them. I told them there were about to be a few changes for the better; that I had met a woman named Lavonica, and I wanted them to meet her and her three daughters. I told them that we planned a picnic at the park for everyone to meet. They were curious about what was planned to take place at the park, so I gave them a few details. They didn't show any kind of rebuttal or ask additional questions. I guess they just decided to go along with it. However, I already knew that it would take Ahmod a while to talk to them because he was very shy.

◆ ◆ ◆

A MESSAGE NOTIFICATION

LAVONICA: Before the weekend came, I sat down with Lady, Bianca, and Makayla and told them all about Tim and his children. I told them how we met and tried to tell them about the sign/confirmation from God. I believe that Lady was the only one who understood, but I wasn't sure if she even cared, being a teenager and all. I was excited that we were getting ready to meet. Also, Tim informed me that I would be meeting his mom, as well. I just kept in mind to be myself. I knew without a doubt that God's hand was on us. I didn't feel the need to be fake or phony. I was going to be authentically me.

It had been a week since I saw him, and I was so ready to be with him in person. It was nice talking on the phone, but so much better in person. Tim and the boys were already at the park and had chosen a picnic table. Tim and I talked about how we thought that it would go with the kids, but I didn't want to put any pressure on them. I was just planning to go with the flow. I figured that Lady and Bianca would be able to hold a conversation, however, I knew Makayla was shy. It would take her a while to warm up to everyone.

So, when the girls and I got out and went to the table. Tim and I hugged each other so tight. I think it was a little weird for all the kids to see us like that we each other. This was the first time the girls had seen me hug another man other than their dad.

We introduced everyone to each other and began to prepare the food to eat. For a moment, it was dead silence between the kids. However, that didn't last long, even Makayla was talking. Ahmod was the last to adjust to us. Halfway through the picnic, he started warming up and talking. Soon enough, everyone was talking, playing games, and running around the park.

It was a pleasure to see Tim interact with his boys and with the girls. Everything just happened naturally. We were getting along like a big happy family. We stayed there for another hour or so and then packed up to go meet Tim's mom, Marion.

TIM: It was Saturday, March 23rd, and they finally made their arrival. I had been counting down to the very minute to see my soon-to-be wife and the girls. Although I never met the girls, it was as though I already knew them because of all the conversations that Lavonica and I had about them. I could tell each one had a unique personality. My goal that day was for everyone to meet each other and have fun together. I was happy because that is exactly what happened. It was a great time!

Previously, I told my mom that Lavonica and the girls were coming over to meet her. It did my heart good to know that the pieces of the puzzle were coming together. Lavonica and the girls were about to see her. She knew that Lavonica was special to me. My mom knew that I didn't introduce anyone to her unless they were special. She was thrilled to meet them. Initially, mom felt that I was moving too fast, but she wanted me to be happy. She questioned me to see if I was sure that I needed someone with kids because she knew that I was already taking care of two kids myself.

I didn't mean to tell his mom that at all.

She felt bringing additional kids to this situation would be even more challenging. I confirmed with her that the Lord's hands were upon us. After that statement, she said she supported us 100%.

◆ ◆ ◆

LAVONICA: I met Tim's mom for the first time and quickly saw that she loved and cared for the well-being of her son. She greeted the girls and me with a big, warm smile and a hug. She made us feel right at home. I didn't know where Tim and the boys were headed, but before I knew it, only the girls and I were in the kitchen with his mom. We began to discuss how Tim and

I met, my background, and things of that nature. Before I realized it, I told her that I loved Tim, and she replied, "But you don't know him." "Oops", I thought to myself. I let it slip again. I didn't mean to tell his mom that! I began to feel the same shame that I felt when I let those words slip out with Tim. This time, however, I took ownership of the statement and *let the chips fall where they may.*

The conversation shifted and the concerned momma in her came out. She began to ask questions about our next move. I could hear the reluctance in her voice and see the resistance in her body language. Her main concern was about how quickly everything was moving with our relationship. Quickly, I explained how God had His hand in our meeting, and I believe with all my heart this was all His doing. She responded with acceptance, and it ended up being a beautiful day with our families.

TIM: My days and nights became longer because whenever I wasn't working, I was either with my boys in Warren or visiting Lavonica and the girls in Hope. Our lives had simultaneously emerged and there were only a few moments when we weren't somehow connected. Our love and conversation had gotten stronger and deeper. The hope or dream of being married one day was no longer far off, we had begun to discuss it regularly. We wanted to be with each other all the time. She shared with me her past, her secrets, and the heartbreak of her mom in the nursing home. I shared with her my past and secrets, as well. We knew that we were healed and delivered from it, and we were starting fresh. We promised not to hold each other victim from the past and that we would not bring old baggage to our relationship.

We continued to move forward in our relationship, and Lavonica wanted me to meet her mom. I had already met her dad, and Lavonica had told him about our supernatural encounter when we first started. He gave us his approval then. She informed me of her mom's situation and shared so many delightful stories with me about being Gladys Tidwell's daughter. The day came when I was able to meet her. We went to Texarkana to the nursing home. Lavonica introduced me and she just smiled. Lavonica said that even though her mom didn't respond, she felt that her mom knew exactly what was taking place. I felt, deep inside, that I made a connection with her mom, and she knew my heart was pure toward her daughter.

◆ ◆ ◆

LAVONICA: I was glad of that moment. I wanted my mom to know that I finally received my true love and that the girls and I would be okay now. Before momma's stroke, she would be concerned about me all the time. She would ask me about my plans for *this* and what would I do about *that*. I wasn't sure if her concern was due to me being the baby girl or if it was due to all the relationship turbulence that I had experienced. Either way, I believe she saw the huge smile on my face along with the peace behind it, just like everyone else saw. Everyone told me how happy I looked to a point that Tim, jokingly, asked me, "What in the world were you looking like at first."

Since we were in Texarkana, we decided to eat dinner at Applebee's (at that time, one of my favorite restaurants). We got seated at our table, and as usual, were having an enjoyable conversation. Suddenly, something unusual took place. It was a moment of pureness, truthfulness, and transparency. *Love is in the air* was the only way I could describe it. No one, not even us, could take credit for this unity. We knew it was all God. We still give God all the glory! We didn't know each other at all, but God knew us. We were two bleeding hearts that were covered by the blood of Jesus that needed to be healed. It was His divine plan that night to let us experience a great love that could only be understood through a relationship with Him, our God.

♦ ♦ ♦

TIM: She was sitting across from me while we were at Applebee's in Texarkana, and I shared with her my heart. I  shared how much she meant to me. I had never been the type to just share my feelings, so this impromptu conversation came from my heart, sincerely. It was something about her that made me feel like I didn't have to suppress or hide my true feelings. I felt comfortable handing her my heart that night. I let down any guard or wall that I had left up. At that moment, it wasn't just about her, it was about me and my trust in God. I trusted God and His plan for me, for us. I sealed that conversation with tears in my eyes for the simple fact that I could easily recognize the hand of God was strongly upon us.

♦ ♦ ♦

LAVONICA: The ride home from Texarkana was peaceful knowing we were in God's direct plan and will for our lives. We ended that great night with a long, loving hug.

The weekend was approaching, and Tim would have Monica and Isaiah visiting him in Warren. The girls and I met them at his mom's house. Isaiah was very laid back and easy to talk with. Isaiah connected with Bianca, I assumed because they were close to the same age. Bianca and Isaiah were like "two peas in a pod" all that day. Now, Ms. Monica is the baby of the group. I could tell that she was used to getting her way. The tiniest one in the family but didn't mind telling me her thoughts and opinions. I remember she said something unacceptable to Makayla that day, and I went to tell Tim about it. He told me that I had to learn how to handle the situation myself. He assured me that I could do it. So, as politely as I could, I explained to Monica that we didn't talk like that to each other, and I told her to apologize. She was remorseful, and she apologized. I instructed them to hug. I was glad that Tim had me deal with it.

Shortly after, Monica and Lady were having a bonding moment. Lady shared with me that she and Monica were in McDonald's restroom in separate stalls. Lady said she started singing Keith Sweat's song lyrics, "Who can love you like me?" and Monica in the other stall replied, "Nobody," completing that part of the song. I had to have laughed so hard from hearing that. Ms. Monica has been my baby ever since.

That same day, we had our first family meeting telling the kids about our next steps and some of our goals for the future.

That meeting would be the first of many. It set the tone and structure of our future family.

♦ ♦ ♦

TIM: When Lavonica notified me that Monica said something inappropriate to Makayla, I felt like I needed to allow her to handle the situation on her own. I knew that she could do it, and I trusted that she would not mistreat any of the kids. I knew if I rescued her from this first dilemma, I would have to do it repeatedly.

We had our seven children there on that day, and reality hit me. We would need a structure for this family to be successful. God put it on my heart to have a family meeting, and I spoke with Lavonica about it. She agreed. That was the day we realized that not only Lavonica and I were chosen, but our family was chosen, put together for a purpose and will of God to accomplish something way bigger than us. We decided on a motto for our family, which was and is "The Chosen Ones" which comes from 1 Peter 2:9 (NLT) – "But you are not like that, for you are a chosen people. You are royal priests, a holy nation, God's very own possession. As a result, you can show others the goodness of God, for he called you out of the darkness into his wonderful light." We ended the meeting with prayer.

♦ ♦ ♦

LAVONICA: Well, everyone had gotten used to me, Tim, and our kids being together all the time. It was not uncommon for them to be at the house all evening until late at night with us. Tywana and her kids had moved out by now, and dad would typically be at the nursing home with mom until 11 p.m. We were able to get a small glimpse of how life would be with just us, together as a family.

After saying our goodbyes one night, Tim and the boys left the house, in his blue Tahoe, and headed home to Warren. It was about 20 minutes later, Tim called me and said they had a flat tire. They ended up getting a hotel room and stayed in Hope. This was the only night we didn't talk his whole drive home. It felt good just knowing that he slept in the same town as me. It probably sounds a little corny now, but those were my true sentiments. Also, that was the night that I learned that the heater in his vehicle had stopped working, and he and the boys bundled up and came to Hope anyway. It showed true commitment, and he wasn't even going to share that with me if it wasn't for getting a flat tire.

♦ ♦ ♦

TIM: All I can say is she was worth it. However, my next visit to Hope was a little different because, for one, I had my daughter, Katlyn, with us to meet Lavonica and the girls. Secondly, I wanted to officially ask Mr. Tidwell if he would give me his blessing to marry his daughter, for him to give me the thumbs up. On the way, I was thinking of different ways how I could ask him. I wasn't nervous, I just wanted to say the

Ahmod (front and center)
(L-R) Jewan, Katlyn, Lavonica, Tim,
Makayla, Bianca, and Lady

right thing. When we arrived, I introduced Katlyn to everyone. I must say that she didn't hesitate to fit right in, especially with the girls. They talked all evening. By now, my boys were calling Lavonica "Momma", and the girls called me "Dad." So, Katlyn followed suit that same night and called Lavonica "Momma." I was glad to see that everyone was getting along so well.

Meanwhile, Mr. Tidwell was at the kitchen table, and I leaned over to ask Lavonica when she thought it would be best for me to talk with her dad. She said now should be good. I asked him if I could talk with him, and he said yes. I went over into the dining room where he was and made it simple. I asked him for his blessing to marry his daughter. I told him my goals and told him that he didn't have to worry about her, that I would treat his daughter right. He said he knew it was the Lord's doing and that he wasn't going to hinder it. In other words, he gave me his

blessings and then proceeded to give me the thumbs up, literally. Immediately, I turned around and gave Lavonica a smile and a thumbs-up. We chitchatted a little more and I went back over into the living room with Lavonica and the kids.

With that hurdle being out the way, that same night Lavonica and I began to discuss a wedding date and where we should live. At that time, we

> *I was able to fall in love with his fatherly side.*

had the option to live anywhere in the United States. We got on the laptop and checked out Bossier City, Louisiana; Texarkana, Texas; Conway, Arkansas; Pensacola, Florida; and Hot Springs, Arkansas. We weighed the pros and cons of them all, but we didn't decide that night.

◆ ◆ ◆

LAVONICA: It was a pleasure finally meeting Katlyn. She was the last one of Tim's children to meet. She was very talkative and was not shy at all. We got along well, and she took plenty of pictures that night with us. That moment was captured, and we can view and remember that day like it was yesterday. Having all the kids around did not change anything about us. If anything, it enhanced my love. We found a way to do family but do us as well. I was able to fall in love with his fatherly side.

Speaking of family, I have always been my daddy's baby girl, so it did my heart good knowing that Tim got the official blessing from my dad. I appreciated Tim wanting that from him. It just showed me his genuine character and the respect he has for his family.

TIM: The next evening approached, and here I was back in Hope again. We were spending so much time together; it had gotten to the point where it was hard for me to leave her. I wanted to be in her presence all the time. So, we had to do it, we had to set a wedding date. We decided on Wednesday, April 10, 2013, that would be the 25th day after we physically meet for the first time.

I found myself thinking about my future with my bride-to-be all the time. We discussed in detail what city would be best for our family to live in. We narrowed it down between Hot Springs, Arkansas, and Bossier City, Louisiana. One thing about it, we did not feel any pressure at that moment because we had previously decided that we would allow the kids to finish school at their current school, being that it was close to the end of the school year before we all moved in together. I knew we had to make vital decisions about our future in a brief period. However, that thought never stressed me or gave me anxiety. Everything just felt right, and I was going along with it.

LAVONICA: We planned for our wedding to be small and intimate. Neither one of us was concerned about all the tiny details, we just knew that we were in love and ready to be together. The most planning we did was selecting a venue (my home church, Faith Temple COGIC) and our wedding colors (brown, which was my favorite color, and Tim chose black). Daddy would officiate, and my brother-in-law, Corey would escort me; and of course, my sister, Tywana, would sing for us. We agreed to have a cake and refreshments, afterward.

Makayla's birthday was March 31st, so we celebrated her eighth birthday on the last weekend. We took Lady, Jewan, Bianca, Makayla, and Ahmod to Bossier City to the Boardwalk and Chucky Cheese. I knew the little ones had fun, but I believed Jewan and Lady did, as well. During that time, we talked with them about being siblings and what that looked like for our blended family. Also, we talked about respecting each other as siblings and as parents. We had to let them know that there would be new rules and a new family structure, but that we would still have fun.

TIM: While in Bossier City, I was observing the kids and seeing how much fun they were having together. I was wondering if

life would be like that once we get married. The Lord did not allow me to overthink or over-complicate anything. I had made up my mind that I would continue to let God order our steps. Also, one of the best things that I love about Lavonica and our relationship was that no matter what was going on, we would still find a way to connect. We did not allow our children to take our full attention from each other.

It was a week before our wedding, and the planning of it consumed our conversations. Not so much planning for the wedding, but conversations about our lives blending together. I shared, excitedly, with my mom all the details. When I told her the wedding date, immediately she checked to see what the weather would be like. After looking it up, she said that it was supposed to storm that day. She regretfully informed me that it would be awfully hard on her to drive to Hope in a storm. It did not take me long to understand my mom's point of view. I felt it would not be any problem with Lavonica agreeing to select another date.

I shared with Lavonica what my mom said about the weather, and she did not have any problem with changing the date. We agreed to have it the day before. So, it was official; we would have our wedding on Tuesday, April 9, 2013, at 7 p.m. Lavonica put out digital invitations and we had a theme called "Love Is In The Air".

Technology has afforded us the ability to capture significant, yet physical moments at any time of the day with our smartphones, digital cameras, and even drones. However, some moments can't be captured with a lens. Those moments can only be etched in our memories. A very brief period consisting of feelings and emotions. We can try out best to depict them with facial expressions or body language, however, that actual feeling itself cannot be seen with the natural eye, only felt. So, when those powerful feelings and emotions grace your presence, enjoy those precious moments.

Chapter 9

Love Is In The Air

When you see a person in love, you don't have to ask them. You see it all in their smile, demeanor, and body language. It is all around them. A person can try to suppress it, hide it, or even try to smother it, but it bursts out while working, talking, walking, and even laughing. Just being in the presence of true love could make the eyes wail with water. Why? Because love is a dimension, it's in the air. It comes with a glow and a specific vibe. When you are around it, love surrounds you, and you can't help but feel it too.

LAVONICA: It was Tuesday, April 9, 2013, and at 7 p.m., I would be marrying the man I had known for 24 days from the first day I met him [March 16th]. The mind-boggling part, I had to work that day. I can't remember one single thing about that workday. My body was there, but my mind was not. I had so many emotions running through my head. I was excited, happy, and anxious. Most of all, I was ready...ready to spend my life with Tim.

We didn't have a decorator, wedding planner, or the formalities traditional involved in weddings. We did have Lawanna "Kay Kay" Griffin cater the food for us, and we ordered our wedding cake from a grocery store in Nashville. Tim's cousin,  Anthony, recorded the service, and my dad officiated it. My brother-in-law, Corey, was my escort, and he was the one appointed to give me away. Lastly, my sister, Tywana, was the soloist.

I made it to Hope from work. I went straight to Kay Kay's house for her to do my hair. She had me looking beautiful! Tim, Ahmod, Jewan, Marion, and Anthony were at mom and dad's house getting ready. Lady, Bianca, and Makayla were there getting ready, as well. I called Tim to let him know I made it to Hope and was getting my hair done. There was excitement in both of our voices. Finally, I made it to mom and dad's house, and yes, Tim saw me before the wedding. We were way past doing things the traditional way! We were all talking, and I shared with them that there was a piece we were missing; Tim never proposed to me. He just told me that he was going to marry me. We skipped that whole part. I guess it was due to how fast everything went. Right then, with no band, orchestra, or blimp with a flag to accompany him, he got down on one knee, in front of the family and asked me to marry him. With a glow, a smile, and a chuckle, of course, I said yes. He got off his knee, gave me that signature smirk and nod, and we hugged.

◆ ◆ ◆

TIM: It was finally our wedding day, and there were a lot of things that needed to be taken care of before the ceremony. I was nervous yet excited about the new journey I was stepping into. It seemed like a long time coming considering the love I had for her. In actuality, however, I found the woman I truly loved and wanted to spend the rest of my life with within less than a month.

On this day, my mind reflected on some of the opinions of others. It reflected on those who asked questions such as "are you sure she is the one," "do you think you are moving too fast,"

It was amazing how you could actually feel the love.

and "do you know her." However, the more I thought about our relationship, the more assured I became. I hadn't even as much kissed this woman, however, I knew that she was my soul mate. I knew, without a doubt, we were supposed to do life together. Those reflective questions dissipated when I reflected on how the prayer we both prayed for each other and how God miraculously showed us our signs.

◆ ◆ ◆

LAVONICA: I arrived at the church my dad pastored, Faith Temple COGIC, in Hope. There were more cars on the parking lot than I excepted. When I entered the church, I noticed that one of the members, Teresa Rollins, had decorated it for us, along with the dining area. It was very unexpected yet beautiful. Our theme was, "Love Is In The Air." It was amazing how you could feel the love. It was, and still is, hard to describe the feeling because it was a God thing. Love saturated the atmosphere. It was no schisms or scams. No "pulling the wool" over anyone's eyes. It was all pure and honest. It was trusting God and taking a leap of faith. It was amazing how you could feel the love.

♦ ♦ ♦

TIM: I was standing at the altar waiting on my bride-to-be. There was no time to be nervous, but I still was. Lavonica told me that it was only going to be a select few attendees, but there were three times that amount! As they stared at me, I had many thoughts that ran through my head. It was a good thing no one could read my thoughts on that  day. One of the thoughts was about "the kiss." I thought about how awkward it would be to kiss her in front of her dad. I must admit, I had quite a few thoughts in this small window of time before our lives changed. I never thought I would be marrying the woman of my dreams this quickly. Another thought was about our honeymoon. Lastly, I just thought about the excitement of the new journey.

♦ ♦ ♦

LAVONICA: I walked through the doors entering the sanctuary to the angelic voice of my sister singing and my handsome husband-to-be waiting on me. My brother-in-law escorted me in. I was a little nervous, but Corey's soft, comforting voice assured me that it was okay to be nervous. He assured me everything would be okay. My dad stood at the altar. Dressed in his clergy attire with his COGIC manual in hand, he was ready to officiate his baby girl's wedding. The people who were present to witness our holy matrimony were all smiles and seemed genuinely happy to be a part of this joyous occasion. They were probably ready to take a glimpse of the first kiss as well because I made it known it would be our first one. The person that stood out the most to me was this tall, handsome, mocha, athletically built man that was waiting for me at the altar; the man who had taken my heart in a matter of days, the man whom I had fallen madly in love with, the man to whom I was willing to give my all to. This man stood there with confidence and regal like it was just him and me in the church. He was my "something GREAT!"

♦ ♦ ♦

TIM: Wow! There she was; walking into the sanctuary, and I realized it was happening. As she walked into the room, the whole atmosphere changed. I looked around and everyone was smiling. I felt that everyone was happy and excited for her, for us. The nervousness quickly went away. I knew without a doubt this woman was planned and purposed for my life. It was amazing how everything felt right and fell into place. There were no thoughts of running, abandoning her, or even saying "I do not." Those 24 days changed me, and I was no longer the same person. I was more than the broken, hurt, confused, misunderstood, divorced, single father.

I stood up there with fearlessness, confidence, and reassurance knowing God had everything under control. I could say, with no hesitation, that she was and still is the woman for me.

◆ ◆ ◆

LAVONICA: During the ceremony, my thoughts weren't too far off from the moment. I was engulfed in the present. I wasn't thinking about what lay ahead, the first kiss, or even the honeymoon. I was focused on the fact that I was about to be married to this God-approved man.

It seemed to take forever to get to the part where the officiator says, "who gives this woman away." It seemed to me that my brother-in-law, whom I love dearly, was by my side for half of the ceremony. That was the only thing that made me kind of fidget, hoping that Dad wasn't going through the vows incorrectly. I kept pointing to Daddy that Corey was still there like he didn't see him. Finally, the moment I was waiting for came, and I was officially given to Tim.

The moment came when I said, "I do", and Dad told Tim, "You may kiss your bride." For a second, I hesitated because my dad was right in front of us, right in our faces. However, that didn't seem to bother Tim one bit! His lips came closer to mine until they touched. It was not a peck or a "kindergarten kiss." It was a kiss that made my inside explode! It was the perfect kiss, the kiss of confirmation. It was like fireworks, church bells, and the angels singing, all wrapped into one. I know the kiss was probably for a few seconds, but it seemed that time stood still. At that moment, I was able to enjoy the best kiss I ever had. I knew I was in for a treat later...I could truly say that the wait was worth it!

◆ ◆ ◆

TIM: We had finally gotten to the part of the ceremony that I had been anticipating and given much thought to...the kiss. Should I give her a peck or a pre-make-out kiss in front of everyone, specifically, her dad? I only had a few seconds to decide what was appropriate. So, I went with my instinct and gave her a kiss she would never forget. A few seconds later, I heard clapping and cheering. I then saw big smiles not only on her face but on the faces of those throughout the church. I knew I made the right decision. I must say that I enjoyed it myself.

◆ ◆ ◆

TIM AND LAVONICA: Congratulations, pictures, and more pictures followed. The food that Kay Kay catered for us was awesome, and the wedding cake was delicious as well. Some good friends and church members decorated the vehicle with the traditional "just married" rituals, which took us by surprise...a good surprise.

The day went by and it eventually got late. We had gotten our kids situated and drove off to enjoy our honeymoon which lasted five days in three states, Louisiana, Texas, and Arkansas.

A MESSAGE NOTIFICATION

♦ ♦ ♦ POST WEDDING ♦ ♦ ♦

LAVONICA: Even though the physical honeymoon was over, we were still honeymooning, and everyone whom we came in contact with told us as much. Love was still in the air. Meanwhile, we had to get situated. Everything went as planned. I continued to work in Nashville and stayed with dad. We planned to do this until the kids got out of school since they only had a month and a half to go. The boys would stay with Tim's mom, and Tim would continue to stay in Hot Springs. We met on the weekends. After school was over, we would start our life in Hot Springs, Arkansas.

♦ ♦ ♦

TIM: Three weeks passed, and I couldn't continue living my life without seeing my wife every day. I tried my best to stick to the plan, however, I decided to go get her. Lavonica made arrangements for Tywana to watch the girls for the next three weeks during the weekday, and we got all five kids on the weekends. Plan B worked, and I was able to enjoy my new bride daily.

A month passed by, and we were all living under one roof in Hot Springs. However, we had one additional person, Isaiah. He wanted to stay with us. Lavonica and I didn't hesitate to agree.

We were considered the "Brady Bunch" with me having three boys and Lavonica having the three girls living with us.

◆ ◆ ◆

TIM AND LAVONICA: We lived like that for about a year. Jewan ended up moving with his mom to Kansas City. So, it left five children. We lived this way for a long while.

As an individual, as a couple, and as a family we

Ahmod, Lady, Makayla, Isaiah, and Bianca

accomplished so many things in the last 9 years. We went on many vacations. We were able to finish college and get our bachelor's degrees, Tim at UAPB and Lavonica at UAM. We owned and operated three clothing stores. We pastored a church for three years in Dumas, AR. We have seen three of our children

graduate from high school and one from nursing school. We have purchased homes and too many cars.

Currently, we are Regional Leaders in the financial services industry. We attend Healing and Deliverance Worship Center in Camden, Arkansas under the leadership of Apostle Keith Marks and Prophetess Claudette Marks. I must say, life has been GREAT! And most of all, LOVE IS STILL IN THE AIR!

Bianca, Monica, Lavonica, Tim, Ahmod, and Makayla

We decided, by the divine will of God, to share these moments with you to show our lives with transparency. Our prayer is that our journey to a beautiful love story brings hope to those who have given up on real love, that it rekindles the love for those for whom love has dwindled, and that it ignites your faith that instant love is possible with and through God. Just know that God is still authoring love stories.

ABOUT THE AUTHORS

Timothy Davis is a born-again believer who loves God and his family with all his heart. He has a Bachelor of Arts in Health and Recreation from the University of Arkansas at Pine Bluff. He is a former pastor of Greater Anointing COGIC in Dumas, AR, and the former State Evangelist with the Arkansas Third Jurisdiction. He is a successful business owner. He loves to spend time with family, evangelizing to others about God, and traveling.

Lavonica Davis is a born-again believer who loves God and her family with all her heart. She has a Bachelor of Arts in Business Administration with a concentration in Marketing from the University of Arkansas at Monticello. She is a business owner, intake coordinator at New Hope Therapy, and the Marketing and Advertising Advisor for Concord Fellowship of Churches International. She loves to spend time with family, graphic designing, reading, and traveling.

Their mission is to give God all the glory in everything they do. They believe in giving everything they do 100%. Their family motto is "The Chosen Ones" - 1 Peter 2:9.

Made in the USA
Columbia, SC
26 January 2023

10669395R00085